PEDRO CALDERÓN DE LA BARCA

WORLD DRAMATISTS

In the same series:

WORLD DRAMATISTS

PEDRO
CALDERÓN
DE LA BARCA

HEINZ GERSTINGER

Translated by Diana Stone Peters

WITH HALFTONE ILLUSTRATIONS

FREDERICK UNGAR PUBLISHING CO.
NEW YORK

Translated from the original German
Text published by arrangement with
Friedrich Verlag, Velber, Germany

CONTENTS

For the convenience of the reader, all play titles are provided in English. Please see bibliography for Spanish titles and translation data.

CHRONOLOGY

1600   Pedro Calderón de la Barca y Barreda Gonzalez de Henao Ruis des Blasco y Riaño is born on 17 January, the middle child among five brothers and sisters. He was descended from an old aristocratic Castilian family. Pedro's father was a court official. His mother was a noblewoman of German descent; her family came from Mons, the capital of the Belgian province of Hainaut, thus the name Henao. She dies in 1610.

1613   Calderón writes his first play, *The Great Bear.*

1615   Calderón's father dies. Calderón attends the Jesuit school in Madrid and is supposed to become a theologian, since the family has a chaplaincy at its disposal. Instead, he studies law, mathematics, and philosophy at the universities of Alcalá and Salamanca.

1622   Calderón wins third prize in a poetry competition. Lope de Vega praises him publicly, since he "at such a tender age has earned laurels which time generally bestows only upon those with white hair."

1625   Calderón becomes a soldier in the service of the *condestable* of Castile. He travels to Italy and Flanders.

1628   Philip IV appoints Calderón court poet and director of the court theater.

1629 Calderón's brother Diego is murdered by an actor. When this actor attempts to find refuge in the Convent of the Trinitarians, Calderón invades the convent together with some of his friends. He is thereupon accused of mistreating nuns.

1635 Calderón becomes the director of the court theater at Buen Retiro.

1636 Two volumes of his dramatic works appear at the instigation of his brother José.

1637 Calderón becomes a knight of the Order of Santiago.

1638 He fights in the battle of Fuenterrabía, when the French try in vain to take this strategically important city.

1640 He fights against the rebellious Catalans. Since Philip IV wishes to keep him at court, he commands him to write a festival play. Calderón completes this work, *The Battle between Love and Jealousy*, within a very short time and returns to the front. Such a return was decreed by the Spanish concept of honor.

1641 Calderón spends this year at the military mission in Madrid.

1642 Calderón is wounded at Constanti and is rendered unfit for battle. He thereupon takes leave of military service.

1645 He receives a monthly pension of thirty gold crowns.

1648 His presumed mistress and the mother of his son Pedro José dies. He himself falls seriously ill.

1651 Calderón becomes a priest. Since he does not get the wished-for chaplaincy in Toledo, he refuses to write for the theater any longer. He does not stick to this decision. (According to some sources this happens in 1645.)

1653　He becomes the chaplain of the Capilla de Reyes Nuevos in Toledo. From there he directs the Corpus Christi plays in Madrid.

1663　He returns to Madrid and becomes Philip IV's honorary almoner. He also becomes a member of the Brotherhood of San Pedro.

1664　The third volume of his dramatic works is published by a friend.

1666　He becomes the superior of the Brotherhood of San Pedro.

1672　The fourth volume of his works appears, with a preface written by himself.

1677　The fifth volume of his works is published, as well as a collection of twelve *autos sacramentales*, which he himself has edited.

1680　He composes a list of his secular plays, which was the basis of the posthumous edition prepared by Juan de Vera Tassis between 1682 and 1691.

1681　On Pentecost Sunday, 25 May 1681, Calderón dies while at work on an *auto*. His friend Solis reports that Calderón died "almost singing, like a swan." At his own request, he was buried in an open coffin in order to illustrate the transitory nature of his body. Three thousand citizens of Madrid follow the funeral procession. His tomb and monument are in the Church of the Savior in Madrid.

CALDERÓN'S AGE
AND HIS WORK

In August Strindberg's *To Damascus*, the last word is "resignation." This resignation meant submission to a higher will, which the individual, after having spent his life in error and insecurity, has come to recognize as the sole authority. Today we see Strindberg not only as one of the fathers of modern drama but also as a writer who has anticipated all of the changes and sufferings of our century. It is precisely in his transformation from a man who seeks into a man who renounces that we can recognize the phenomenon that not only provides us with a mirror image of our spiritual and intellectual development but also exemplifies the theater of our age: the subordination of the psychological drama of character by a new kind of theater. The human being as an individual returns the initiatives for his actions to a power outside of himself. He no longer acts; rather, he is acted upon. If we substitute for Strindberg's resignation, Calderón's word *desengaño*, literally disillusionment, a striking parallelism can be observed. *Desengaño* also means an awakening from illusion and the recognition of a higher will. That this higher will was of a strictly determined kind in the Catholic Calderón distinguishes his work only in degree from today's. From a dramaturgical point of view, both kinds of theater arise from the same presuppositions.

With this perspective in mind we can examine the way in which the so-called strange Calderón affects our own age in a most striking and exciting way. Calderón is fascinating not merely because he is strange and remote, as Hugo Friedrich, the most important Calderón scholar of our age, believes. This may hold true for a purely literary consideration of this writer. A theatrical analysis of Calderón must, however, recognize his relevance, though it seems that Calderón scholarship as a whole is concerned with Calderón the poet, not Calderón the dramatist.

For the theatergoer, a sympathetic understanding of history is, at most, only of secondary interest. A play that requires a historical commentary possesses no inherent life of its own. It also contradicts the theatergoer's basic demand for the portrayal of a realistic present, regardless of what age or what culture has given rise to the play being performed. That Calderón was not only a theatrical specialist but over and above this, a man of learning, is proved both by his manifold studies and, in another area of art, by his interest in painting, a subject he wrote about in his mature years.

1. Spain's Golden Age

The world that lay behind Calderón, in which he lived and wrote, seems a strange one to us today.

Spain, which even now is an outsider apropos of Europe, is isolated from other countries of western Europe by more than the Pyrenees. Though its internal and external history has been far more independent than that of other European nations, Spain has served as a reflector of events that at other times and under different circumstances took place in other parts of the western world.

At the time of Calderón's birth, Philip III, a third Hapsburg monarch, sat on the throne of Spain. Under his predecessor, Philip II, Spain had reached the height of its short-lived but mighty power—and this had occurred within a century from its birth as a nation when the two states of Castile and Aragon were united following the marriage of Ferdinand and Isabella in 1469. In 1492, Abdallah, the last Moorish king, had returned to Africa after Granada was conquered by Isabella. In the same year Columbus had founded Haiti, the first Spanish colony in America. Through the Hapsburg succession, The Netherlands had become Spanish provinces. In 1559, the perpetual wars between France and Spain had ended in victory for Spain. In 1571, Don Juan de Austria, the half-brother of Philip II, had destroyed the Turkish fleet near Lepanto, thus assuring Spain's predominance in the Mediterranean. In 1580, as a result of the extinction of its own royal house, Portugal had fallen to Spain by default.

But the very next year, 1581, with the secession of The Netherlands, the decline of Spanish power began. Seven years later the Spanish Armada was defeated off the coast of England. In 1648, the republic of The Netherlands was officially recognized.

More important even than these events was what

was happening within Spain, a process that stands in more glaring contradiction to that in the rest of Europe. The extreme poverty from which the Spanish population had suffered for centuries could not be alleviated even through the greatest successes in foreign policy. Even if the Spanish kings, especially Charles V, succeeded in limiting the power of the nobility by giving knights high places at court and thus binding them to the center of power, it must not be forgotten that these Spanish aristocrats were not capitalists as many of their counterparts in France were. Centuries of guerilla warfare with the Moors had prevented the Spanish nobility from resting in peace. (These Moors, who had managed to establish a flourishing nation, were far more tolerant and socially just than their "Christian" successors from Andalusia.) The knights remained crusaders on their own initiative. Because the power of the Moors prevented the Spaniards from obtaining material goods, honor and religious belief became all-important to them, attributes to be defended at all cost.

For their part, the common people, having long been accustomed to war and misery, looked upon their own wretchedness not as a matter of social injustice but as a matter of divinely ordained fate. Liberation from misery could come only as promised by the Catholic church, and thus they defended this religion passionately against all those who believed differently. In this ambiance, it was easy for the clergy to establish the rule of power that made religious change or innovation impossible for centuries to come. But it would be wrong to evaluate Spanish Catholicism and its political power only from this materialistic point of view. Such a viewpoint would make such people as Saint

Theresa of Avila and Ignatius Loyola incomprehensible. The passion inherent in the Spanish national character expressed itself equally in the military ambition of the aristocracy and the unconditional asceticism of the saints. At the beginning of the seventeenth century, earthquakes, floods, and pestilence led to social catastrophe. In 1624, the year of inflation, a third of Spain's civil servants had to be dismissed. In 1640, the first social revolution broke out in Catalonia because of unjust oppression through taxation.

But neither Spain's political heyday under Philip II nor the total economic collapse under his successors altered the people's basic attitude. It is true that the conversion from knightly service to court service had produced changes in the aristocracy. The rule of the day dictated the acquisition of as much material wealth as possible at the cost of the small peasant. Any kind of work was considered to be undignified. And the concept of honor was transformed from that of a knightly ideal to that of an aristocratic mode that caused much bloodshed. In peculiar contradiction to this autocratic concept stood the selfless loyalty of this aristocracy to the king, who, alone in seventeenth-century Europe, was still recognized as ruling by divine right. One can hardly speak of a middle class in Spain similar to that which had begun to emerge at this time in other countries of Europe. The peasant class was severely limited in its rights both by the infringements of the nobility as well as by a special authorization of the king, which prohibited them from establishing a bourgeois court system. Benito de Pensalosa y Mondragón, a contemporary of Calderón, composed a graphic report about the social condition of the peasants. Among other things, he wrote:

The peasant class is at present the poorest, the most wretched, the most abject and lowly class in Spain; indeed, it seems as if all the other classes had united and conspired together to ruin and destroy it. The situation has gone so far that the very name peasant has such a bad name that it is synonymous with villain, lout, dirty fellow and still worse. If one says peasant, one thinks of coarse food, dishes prepared with garlic and onions, of barley loaves, and of the meat of animals that have died. One thinks of shoes made of un-tanned leather, of torn tunics, of fool's hoods and coarse capes, of burlap shirts and shapeless carry-ing bags, of semi-decayed clay hovels, a scrap of poorly tilled earth, a few scrawny cows, and the burden of mortgages, interests, taxes, and levies. Should the peasant come to town . . . only endless disappointments await him . . . but he becomes a true martyr as soon as court officials or soldiers find their way into his modest hut.

Thus the lower classes remained pretty much a composition of tradesmen, itinerant craftsmen, jour-neymen, conjurers, vagabonds, and last but not least, a well-organized group of thieves who existed on good terms with the corrupt police and were also used by many a great man as paid accomplices. That the clergy, both monks and nuns, were legion in Spain during the sixteenth and seventeenth centuries is well enough known.

The most distinct difference between Spain and its neighboring countries at this time was to be seen in its spiritual and intellectual life. The profound transfor-mation of European culture, which the Renaissance and the Reformation had effected in the rest of Europe, did not touch Spain. It is precisely in the so-called classical works of Calderón that we can recognize how little he was influenced by classical antiquity. The ancient world was to him no more than one exotic subject among others. The frequent designation of Spain as the birthplace of the counterreformation is accurate only apropos of Spain's relations with foreign countries. Within Spain itself, one can scarcely speak of a counterreformation, since it never experienced a Reformation. Least influenced by the Reformation were its artists, whose religious works were never tendentious, neither in a militant nor a didactic sense.

The Inquisition was originally directed against the Muslims and the Jews, but its persecution of all non-Catholics was preeminently a matter of national political policy, because it was feared that every non-Catholic was really a secret ally of one of the northern powers. The diabolical cruelty of the Inquisition is therefore the first excess that was committed in Europe for nationalist ends.

Alone in seventeenth-century Europe, Spain remained Catholic in a medieval sense, retaining the medieval belief in the beatific church, one that guaranteed order both in this world and in the next. Spain's participation in the Thirty Years' War signified the last fight of the retreating spirituality of the Middle Ages against the increasingly materialistic orientation that in Richelieu's France was dictating national policy.

The monarch who recognized Calderón's genius and to whom Calderón owed his offices and his fame was Philip IV. The loyalty of the nobility and of the people was directed toward his office, not toward his person. As a political man he was a weakling who completely entrusted his tasks to others. But these people could no longer hold back the decline of the Spanish empire. Philip IV's religious views no longer were imbued with the passion that had permeated the religion of Philip II. Moreover, in his personal life Philip IV was hardly an exemplar of Catholic morality. He had numerous mistresses and illegitimate children; for a while, his mistress, the actress Maria Calderona, wielded political power. But in this he hardly differed from the rest of the aristocracy. Whether married or not, it was customary for a nobleman to have a mistress whom he guarded as jealously as he did his lawfully wedded wife. Philip IV's life and love, however, were primarily devoted to art. And since this love was not merely the pose of the patron peculiar to princes, a matter of prestige that is, but was a matter of genuine understanding, he did more for his country—speaking from the perspective of a later age—than did his politically more significant predecessors. Through Philip IV, Spain's age of political decline has come down to us as the golden age of Spanish literature.

2. Spanish Theater in the Golden Age

Though they were patrons of all protecting the fine arts, Spanish kings particularly patronized the theater. If a king wrote plays himself or acted in them, this was not to be seen in terms of ego motives, which probably provided the moving force for Nero or Louis XIV, both of whom are said to have written and acted in plays. Rather, the theatrical *engagement* of Spanish royalty was an expression of the essential nature of a people for whom theater fulfilled a deep need.

It is true, Philip's financial expenditure for his theater presented a terrifying contrast to the poor social condition of his country. It also stands to reason that foreign artists, above all Italian stage architects, did not come to Spain simply for the sake of glory. To cite only one example, the production of an operetta in the pleasure palace of Zarzuela cost sixteen thousand ducats.

The interweaving of theater and religion was a particularly Spanish characteristic. In northern Europe, a Christian theater had developed only after laboriously liberating itself from liturgical forms. In Spain the Christian forms of worship had remained within the tradition of pagan custom, since they had from the very beginning included both dance and mime. Even the various temporary prohibitions handed down from time to time did not succeed in banning these forms from the church. The priest was not considered an administer of a religious rite. Rather, he was identified with Christ during the mass in the same way that an actor is identified with his role. This is not unlike the situation that exists today in Spain where the statues of saints are honored not as sacred images but as incarnations of the saints themselves. Religious festivals provided welcome occasions for great pageantry. The introduction of the feast of Corpus Christi by Pope Urban IV in 1264, with its great procession of the Host, offered to all forms of theater the greatest variety of possibilities.

The secular form of theater appears to have developed primarily from the courtly romances, which were performed in mime by singers and buffoons. The oldest extant dramas clearly reveal the presence of this epic form; for this reason they were long thought of as narratives in dialogue form. The Spaniards' pleasure in all forms of display and their glorification of "noble" passions led to a special kind of theatrical art, which developed soon after a politically more stable state emerged through the union of Ferdinand and Isabella. After an era characterized by itinerant theater —an era of theater not unlike that existing elsewhere in Europe, despite the fact that contemporary reports contain much strange material—Spanish actors had, within a century, progressed from a position of social ostracism to one of highest regard at court. It is of note that in contrast to other countries actresses were permitted to appear on the stage even in the early days of professional theater. Theater had become the fashion in Spain around 1600.

The stage that Calderón found at hand had long outgrown the primitive phases of its infancy. There was already a court theater and a folk theater. Although these two types of theaters differed both structurally and socially, the same dramatists wrote plays for both of them. Luis Cabrera tells us though that their majesties wished to have a theater in which they could see plays performed exactly as they were being put on in the *corrales* of the people; they expected to derive more pleasure from them in this way than they could get from troupes putting on plays in the chambers of their own palaces. Therefore, the court in Madrid had acquired a folk theater in addition to its own theater in the days of Philip II.

The structure of the folk theater was approximately as follows: The boards of the stage were set up in a *corral* (courtyard) and surrounded on three sides by

wagons. On these wagons were constructed the properties necessary for the various *jornadas* of the play,
that is, the "days." Later, a *jornada* became an act of a
play. There were trapdoors and hoisting apparatuses
of various degrees of sophistication, depending on the
financial state of the troupe. The *corrales* were rented
out to the itinerant troupes by the various sodalities.
The theatergoers paid a double entrance fee, one to
the actors, one to the sodality. Hospitals, old-age
homes, even schools, were supported by these sodalities rather than by the state.

The windows of nearby houses were used as loges,
and benches were set up as in a stadium. Between them
and the stage lay the patio, or that area from which a
large and noisy claque (the *mosqueteros*) vociferously
settled the fate of the play. Even the best dramatists
were at their mercy. For this reason most Spanish
plays concluded with a plea to the audience for its
indulgence.

The acting troupes were highly unequal, both socially and artistically. If we can give credence to the
yarn-spinning reports of Agustín de Rojas (1602),
there were eight various types of troupes ranging
from the *bululu*, an itinerant solo actor, to the *com-
pañia*, a large theatrical company that was both highly
placed socially and economically well organized. The
autos sacramentales, plays celebrating specific religious
events, of which Calderón wrote many fine ones, were
performed by the same actors who presented the secular plays. Obviously only the best troupes were invited
to perform at the court theater. Originally similar also
in its external structure to that of the folk theater, the
court theater came under the influence of the Italian
baroque theater during the reign of Philip IV and his

theatrical director, Calderón. This new architectural structure was appropriate to the primary function of the court theater, which was, namely, to offer impressing plays for visiting guests. It is to Calderón's credit that, through his direction and through his plays, he prevented the court theater from declining into mere pageantry. Immediately after his death came the triumph of crude and boorish theater, adventure drama, and the *zarzuelas*, a Spanish form of light opera. Calderón understood how to serve the tastes of his age without compromising himself.

In 1635, Calderón became the director of the court theater of Buen Retiro. According to reports that have been passed down to us, this theater with wings was constructed in the Italian style. It exceeded even most Italian theaters of the day in its technical refinements and ingenious devices. The auditorium represented a courtly transformation of the *corrales* of the folk theater. The loges, as in the *corrales* theater, were windows. There were seats only for the ladies; gentlemen stood up. The theater was illuminated by wax torches.

The architects of this theater, who were also its permanent set designers were the Italians Cosme Lotti (whom the Spaniards called a sorcerer), Cesare Fontana, and later on, the still more ingenious Baccio del Bianco. It was, however, the background that fundamentally distinguished this stage from those in Italy. It was a platform on which mountains as well as heaven and hell could be shown. By opening the back wall the park was revealed to the audience. Here mass entrances, peasant riots, and battles could be realistically portrayed. We cannot even begin to imagine the technical subtleties of this theater. It met all of the

demands of a baroque "magic theater." Lope de Vega
(Lope Félix de Vega Carpio) complained as early as
1629 that this theater forced "our ears to be subordinated so that our eyes are feasted."

Calderón, so it is said, was terrified that first time he
saw Baccio del Bianco's theater. During the year in
which he was appointed director of this theater, the
premiere of his *Love, The Greatest Enchantment* took
place in the park of the palace. On the basis of the
detailed reports concerning this premiere, we can
draw some conclusions as to the nature of these outdoor performances in general. The effects of storms at
sea were produced in the park's ponds by means of
invisible paddle wheels; whole islands sank in the
water; tritons and nixes swam in the waves. To top it
all off, the audience was offered the spectacle of fish
spurting streams of perfumed water. It seems to us
today to be a miracle that the poetic word was not lost
in the midst of all this. As Ludwig Pfandl says of Calderón: "It is as though he had two types of spectator
in mind; as if he had to do the thinking for the one
and the artistic writing for the other; as if he had to
conceal his more profound thoughts modestly behind
superficial trifling so that only the initiated would perceive them."

To create a level space on which to construct this
outdoor theater, which was afterward in constant use,
an entire mountain was removed. At one end of this
tree-surrounded area the stage was erected and at the
other end a balcony for spectators. Twelve hundred
wax torches and glass lanterns provided illumination.

The performances of Calderón's works in Buen
Retiro may be counted among the rare blissful hours in
theatrical history. Spectacle, acting, and poetry were

combined in such perfection as has rarely ever been achieved. These plays also represented Spain's last and most passionate expression of its medieval ideal of an empire that was to represent an allegory for the divine realm. Calderón's theatrical world has been termed *orbe perfecto*; his works as parallels of the Spanish concept of empire time and again depicted "variants of the cosmos as a whole as seen from different perspectives."

3. Calderón's Dramaturgy

Distrust of Calderón's dramatic form stems from the reaction of the last two generations against the false pathos of postromanticism. By postromanticism we do not mean only the watered-down romantic literature of the late-nineteenth century, which still exerts its baneful influence in popular stories, cheap novels, and expensive films. We also mean the inclination of a particular level of society in an age to veil with aesthetic ornament and sentimentality the terrifying and disillusioning conditions of reality. This tendency can be seen in religious platitudes as well as in moral sob stuff, in nationalistic posing as well as in political rhetoric. A generation that has suffered from the realization of such rhetoric has good reason to be skeptical of every kind of bombast and pomposity. It is the same skepticism that determined Christian Friedrich Grabbe's creative process, a skepticism that a hundred years ago gave rise to a realistic form of art as a reaction against romantic pathos. The naturalistic theatrical style as well as the understatement that prevailed in the 1950s also expressed this fear of dishonesty. Moreover, this

fear of deception extends even to our very own feelings; we prefer to disguise them with irony rather
than display them directly.

It is very difficult to make clear to such a skeptical
generation the distinctions that exist between dissimu-
lated and real emotion, between false and genuine
theatricality. To get back to Calderón, let us recall
Goethe's assertion that the intellectual content of Calderón's "plan is comprehensible to the intellect." And
although analyzing Calderón's baroque form in the lim-
its of this book will be difficult, such analysis
will enable us moderns to appreciate the beauty of his
work.

The language of Calderón's plays, characterized by
the individuality and multiplicity of Spanish verse
forms, was long subject to criticism for being bombastic. Eugen Gürstner, a translator of Calderón, is of
the opinion that Calderón can be won for the modern
stage only through the spirit of his language. This
would mean then that since all translations are to some
extent inadequate, Calderón is unplayable in all but
Spanish theaters. Gürstner further asserted that the
lyrical quality of Calderón's language is more important than its meaning and its psychological aspects. A
vital handling of Calderón's works would then be impossible outside of the Spanish-speaking world, since
every language has its own lyricism. But Gürstner is
right in insisting upon a faithful translation. For if
Calderón's language is lost in the process of translation, a basic element, if not *the* basic element, of his
work disappears.

Calderón's language reveals an inclination characteristic of our own age: i.e., the elimination of nature
as a subject is also characteristic of modern lyric

poetry. It is no accident that two of our greatest modern poets became disciples of one of Calderón's contemporaries; a poet who for a long time was simply dismissed as bombastic, Luis de Góngora y Argote. Paul Verlaine wanted to translate his work, and Federico García Lorca called him the father of modern lyric poetry. If Calderón has now and again been accused of gongorism, such an accusation but reaffirms the affinity of his verbal manner of expression to that of our own times. He describes things by means of bold metaphors. Metaphorically he transforms things into something completely different. For example, nowhere in *Life Is a Dream* is a horse ever called a horse; rather, the word horse is always presented in poetic code. This technique derives not only from Calderón's joy in punning, but also from his delight in metaphorical transformation. The dramatist handled his characters with all the freedom of his imagination. In so doing, he revealed his fondness for expressing natural images in terms of artificial ones and artificial ones by natural ones.

To cite one example, Calderón described Semiramis's hair in twenty-six lines of verse in *The Daughter of Air*. A passage such as this is not undramatic and bombastic verse but rather extremely clever poetry created by a very imaginative intellect. Actually, such passages are necessary because they serve to create the consciously unreal, antinaturalistic atmosphere of his plays. They correspond to the stucco decoration employed by baroque architecture: this decoration is not unintegrated adornment but a very characteristic part of the composition as a whole.

The construction of Calderón's plays is directed wholly toward theatrical effectiveness. But this structure is not meant to produce mere empty effects. It exists in an intimate relationship to Calderón's world view. His dramatic structure does not correspond to the familiar psychological construction of classical dramaturgy—a lack that was long held to be a failing. Even Calderón's own compatriots imputed to him the error of having failed to depict consistent and logical characters. In the 1880s, the Spanish scholar Marcelino Menéndez y Pelayo bemoaned the fact that Calderón succeeded in only once portraying a consistent character, and this in *The Mayor of Zalamea*. Like most of his contemporaries, Menéndez y Pelayo overlooked the fact that Calderón's theatrical figures are passive heroes, not active heroes, because they are not anthropocentrically conceived; the center of the world lies not within them but outside them. Calderón was not concerned with immediate observation of life nor with its graphic representation. Rather, he was concerned with the allegorical reproduction of life. Thus he remained completely within the artistic tradition of the Middle Ages. This concept of art that characterizes his work also connects him to our modern age. This becomes clear when we freely adapt the concept of Calderón's allegory to our own concept of abstraction.

The dramaturgical order of his plays is governed neither by the logical nor the psychological; nor is it ruled by the free play of his imagination, as has been wrongly assumed. Calderón's work is dominated entirely by a specific cosmic meaning. The starting point of his plays always involves a drama of human powers. The theatrical genius of Calderón is demonstrated by the fact that graphicality prevails in precisely those areas where the play's action becomes spiritual. It can be transformed into the most passionate kind of theatrical effect, but it nevertheless always remains within the boundaries of aesthetic moderation. Culture rather than nature informs his work. August Wilhelm Schlegel knew of no other dramatist "who understood so well how to poeticize dramatic effect and who was at the same time so graphic, so forceful, and so aesthetic."

Calderón's ability to transform spiritual abstraction into luxuriantly graphic effect on the stage is at the heart of the particular art of his dramaturgy. This art remained unrecognized for a long time since critics only wanted to see the plays' baroque dress and their theological purpose. But it is precisely because Calderón was able to convert abstraction into theatrical effect that he serves as an example for modern theater. After the aridity of discussion plays, contemporary drama once again strives for logical abstraction as well as for optical and acting effects.

Even allegory, which is essentially an abstraction, becomes graphic in Calderón's works. It becomes the individual bearer of ideas. That Calderón dealt freely with historical or mythological material is typical of the prevailing spirit of his age. His creative process obeyed an exclusively dramatic law, which is in itself a reflection of a higher cosmic law. Thus, to those who reproach Calderón for his so-called bombastic language, we can offer in response the rigorously thought-out cast of his style, his cosmically determined dramaturgy, and finally, his theatrical genius, which is able to make the spiritual perceptible through the senses.

It seems in order here to make a few observations about the gracioso, the serving man, who appears so frequently in Calderón's comedias. Though the noble master and his comical sidekick are timeless types in world theater, we must not assume that all of these figures are identical in all epochs and in the works of all dramatists. Social and personal points of view play an important role in their characterization. Their primary function is purely theatrical; for the contrast between these two types is in itself of striking dramatic effect. The gracioso is both timid and, in comparison with his master, pathetic in countenance. And yet, he often possesses more common sense than his master when it comes to the ordinary affairs of life. The servant's words are a burlesque play on the words of the hero.

But while the contrast in itself is crucial in the works of other dramatists, Calderón is more concerned with the complementary nature of this relationship. His conception of cosmic order is never onesided. The world is not entirely heroic, but neither is it wholly comical. Likewise, human activity may not result only from idealism, but realism is not its only motivation either. The relationships here are complementary. That is to say, Calderón's comedy is not "a comedy of contrasts but one of complements." His graciosos are not absolutely identical to the harlequins of other countries. For Calderón, the gracioso's freedom to act the fool is as limited as is all human freedom. While the freedom of the graciosos has all sorts of possibilities for expression within the realm of social affairs, it is restricted in the ethical sphere. Foolishness in Calderón's works does not mean license to circumvent the laws, as is true in many other areas of literature. The gracioso, too, is subordinate to these laws. In *The Phantom Lady*, Cosme is still a buffoon, though the gracioso is characterized in many ways in other plays.

4. *Calderón's World View*

To us today, Calderón's world view seems even more alien than his dramaturgy. Though his politics and his religion are basically inseparable—since the Spanish kingdom was thought to be a microcosm of God's realm—we shall look at them as separate items. The almost divine worship of kings is clearly limited in Calderón's plays to Spanish kings. Foreign monarchs, from history or legend, are treated by the dramatist like any ordinary mortals. The Spanish king appears not on the stage as a person, but rather as a personified idea, as the idea of order and justice. The king performs the function of the Greek *deus ex machina*, but his presence has more significance than this. For the dramatist is concerned not only with poetic justice but with real justice, which can also be called grace in the Christian world. The king, who finally intervenes at the end of the play and creates order out of the confusion that is always present in the Calderón plot, symbolizes the cosmic principle according to which everything has meaning and in which everything comes to rest.

The perplexity with which modern directors eye the entrance of the king in the last act of *The Mayor of Zalamea* is the result of the fact that this play has received more critical consideration than most of the other plays. It is generally thought of as a realistic folk play. But even the plot of *The Mayor of Zalamea* was an allegory for Calderón, an example of the adventure of human life in which the Spanish king, as representative of God, finally recalled all of the players to their fixed and rightful positions within specific boundaries.

It is much more difficult for us to comprehend the concept of honor, the overestimation of a single virtue that often does not even seem like a virtue to us. Honor as a theme in Calderón's work has manifold faces—it ranges from a matter of religion to a parody of social convention.

Joseph von Eichendorff wrote: "In Calderón's works love is unconditionally subordinate to honor and honor is consecrated by religion, which for Calderón is love." This sentence does not apply only to Calderón. Rather it characterizes the world view that prevailed in the Spain of his day. As in so much else, Calderón acts as the principal poetic interpreter of an entrenched idea. In one of his plays, he writes, "Great ambition for honor is not ambition for gain"—and this sounds like a defense. Aside from the fact that the concept of honor was more than just highly esteemed in all those lands (from Iceland to Japan) in which knighthood existed, honor was the single value worth striving for in Spain in the early centuries of Christianity. For in that age, such other goals as the acquisition of permanent material wealth or the establishment of power were illusions due to the unstable conditions produced by incessant war.

In this period there arose, then, that unique overestimation of the concept of honor that spread throughout all levels of society including the stratum of the common people. It was to degenerate in a craze for duels that were not even punishable by law in which death as a result of some trifling affair was an everyday occurrence.

Today we find Calderón's tragedies, in which the code of honor is exemplified and followed through to its ultimate consequences, cruel and repellent. It is astonishing that this same dramatist wrote a play about the last permitted duel in Spain and condemned it— but only late in his life after a royal decree put a stop to dueling. We cannot know whether Calderón himself had come to some new insight concerning this matter or whether the play was merely a reflection of the royal will.

In any case, it is solely the Spanish concept of honor that prevents us from properly appreciating today the work and world of Calderón. The Romance scholar James Fitzmaurice-Kelly maintained that it was Calderón's "race, his religious belief, and his environment which prevents him from becoming a world dramatist of universal significance." It is my opinion, however, that it is only the concept of honor, common to all three of the aspects mentioned by Fitzmaurice-Kelly, that really remains as a perpetual obstacle to our appreciation of Calderón. If the German journalist who claims to recognize as the basic characteristic of Calderón's work the fact that the human being develops not according to his inherent character but instead is solely determined by the law of honor is right, then the spirit of Calderón's total work is indeed limited. But as I see it, honor by no means provides the exclusive internal or external determinant of Calderón's work despite the great significance it held for him. The concept of honor is either a part of or is actually merged in that fundamental religious idea that we can characterize by means of the title of Calderón's play, *Life Is a Dream.*

5. Catholicism in Calderón's Plays

"Even for us Catholics," wrote Heinrich Laube, a nineteenth-century theater director, in his memoirs, "this world of Spanish thought seems both strange and constricting; we have long since outgrown it in our own literature." In his eyes then the Catholicism of later ages has only little in common with the Catholicism of Calderón's own day. But such a point of view runs counter to the very core of Catholicism, a religion that has always modified only its form but never its inner structure.

Catholicism is the order and the cosmos in which Calderon's world view resides. For Calderón there is no other possible faith. His works were meant not as battle cries against religious reformers and rationalists, as the works of contemporary Jesuits were. Because his cosmos represented the universal stage of a theater in which the drama of life took place, he had no need to defend it. All non-Catholic spheres, such as classical antiquity, paganism, Judaism, and Islam, are seen as preliminary steps toward Christianity, as seeds which contained within themselves all the potential from which the fully developed plant emerged. This idea is expressed not only in Calderón's religious plays but also in his secular ones, though its clearest expression can be found in the *autos sacramentales*, which "elevate the classical myth to give it salvation through the mystery of Christianity" (Hugo Freidrich). Critics tend to deny that Calderón had a philosophy of his own. They evaluate the intellectual content of his works as formulations of the spirit of his age. It is well here to keep in mind the fact that Calderón occupied himself intensively with philosophical and theological problems and that he experienced the spirit of his age actively and passionately as a soldier and as a priest.

The equation that life is a dream—which Calderón himself left in uncertainty by asking whether it was not a dream to say that life is a dream—corresponds to the baroque religiosity of the Spanish people. The asceticism of Spanish saints was not a frantic renunciation of the world, not a mortification of the flesh out of hate for the body. Instead it was an act resulting from the knowledge that existence in an uncertain and transitory world makes all men into uncertain and transitory beings simply by virtue of their belonging to such a world. Moreover—and this corresponds to the graphic representation of spiritual values peculiar to Spanish theater—this asceticism also represented the saint's dionysian exultation over his proximity to God, the single absolute being in a world of illusion. As José Ortega y Gasset has written: "The mystical ecstasy of the monks and the nuns of that age has nothing to do with contemplation."

The artistic form that gave expression to this dream-like and uncertain world was that of baroque illusion. This conscious form of illusion, which also dominated the theater, stands diametrically opposed to the naturalistic illusion of the nineteenth century. In the nineteenth century, one attempted to portray illusion as if it were reality; in Calderón's age, one attempted to portray reality as if it were an illusion. If, for example, a baroque painting seems so real that we feel as though we could enter inside it, this is intended not only as illusion, but also as disillusion, for the very next moment we step up close to the painting, the illusion of sensual perception is canceled by the disillusion by the intellect. This phenomenon is artistically expressed through the theme that life is a dream. With this, however, the baroque theater of illusion, now recognized as a theater of disillusion, approaches the theater of our age. "Then go and adorn those glorious illusions with prodigal agility so that each man may think he is observing reality," says the Master in *The Great World Theater* to Madame World. This fundamental concept of baroque art has hardly ever been expressed so simply and so clearly.

For Calderón, if the human being wishes to avoid despair, given the absolutely uncertain nature of his existence, his only choice is to recognize a higher power that resides outside of him. For Calderón, it is the recognition of the divine will. As he wrote, for example, in *The Loud Secret*: "To submit to fate means to deprive fate of its victory." This reveals that Calderón had taken the classical concept of fate into the Christian world. It can be said still more precisely: Calderón identified fate with God's will. This point of view is not new. It corresponds to medieval philosophy, which taught at the same time what seems to us to be a strange dependence of fate upon astrological configurations. Of course, the origins of this concept lie much further in the past, in a magical world view, which shows up both in Calderón's works as well as in those of our own day, although in forms that differ externally.

The human being's subjection to fate provides one of the most basic dramatic themes in the literature of all ages. The only variable is the way in which different human beings respond to their fate. It would be false to equate Calderón's fate dramas with those of antiquity. For Calderón, human life is entirely unpredictable, for even the fate that has been effected by the stars can at any time be changed by the will of a personal God. As Karl Vossler wrote: the Spanish comedia strives above all to depict the "unpredictability of all things" and with this, the fact that "chance is not an exception but the rule and that all life is an adventure."

Life seen as a chain of adventures necessarily precludes causal laws. But life does offer the human being two ways of surviving: the individual can struggle to acquire power and thus possibly become the master of his life or he can take the sting out of fate by recognizing his own impotence. The second alternative is the right one for Calderón. The first possibility, in his view, rests on a fallacy, since the real power, which man thinks he is obtaining, is an illusion like all so-called reality. What is absolute, however, is God's will or the cosmic order. To recognize God's will is to make man into a part of the cosmos and to give him a share in the absolute.

But this view of life has nothing to do with fatalism. Neither was it influenced by the Mohammedan concept of kismet, as many scholars assume. It is Christian because of its particular interpretation of fate, which includes both the temptation to commit sin as well as the possibility of grace. Sin and grace only exist, however, within the context of human free will. To explain the function of human free will within the framework of a religion whose principles depend upon the unconditional recognition of cosmic order as

God's will is the most urgent concern of Calderón's religious drama.

The problem of free will formed the center of philosophical and theological discussion during Calderón's student years at Salamanca. "The human being has no freedom so long as he belongs to the world as one natural being among others; he has freedom only when he rises above nature and joins himself to God" (Max Kommerell). It has been left to man himself to determine his inner life, though not his external life: for "neither magic nor affliction can master the free will." Calderón quite unequivocally formulates this point of view through the words of the Master in *The Great World Theater*: "I could have corrected much that was wrong in the world, but instead I gave the human being strength of will and dominion over his passions, so that each man could diligently strive through his own actions to ennoble himself." That the ultimate decision for his own life is left to man himself, can be seen in a quotation from *The Daughter of Air*: "For this I do know, though I know but little; that heaven never in an ungodlike manner forces our decision."

This free will may now decide between the two above-mentioned possibilities. Either man falls victim to temptation and sin by recognizing worldly power as the highest authority, or he places his own will at the service of a higher will. In the first case, he chooses that which is transitory, a mere nothing, and becomes nothing himself. In the second case, he steps in to preserve the Catholic order. But, to be sure, it is a Catholic order that does not spend itself in ephemeral matters. Instead this Catholic order is conceived of as representing a moral order both within the individual and in society as a whole. The ultimate and highest form of decision that the human free will can make is total renunciation of the world and preparation for God through asceticism and consecration. Ultimately, the choice of these alternatives is, in Calderón's sense, a succinct expression of the choice between reality and illusion.

The direct intervention of God in the life of each individual is that act of grace that also provides the dramatically decisive point in Calderón's dramas. Whether or not man accepts this act of grace and what he does with it—this is the content of human action both in the drama of life and on the stage. The fact that this granting of grace is symbolized through the miracle of the sacraments is a reflection of the general tendency of Catholicism as a whole and of baroque theater in particular to make the spiritual graphic. Therefore, Calderón and his contemporaries felt impelled to go beyond the mere intellectual presentation of the theme of grace; and this they accomplished by presenting in visual equivalents an act of grace through the use of the sacraments on the stage. Secular plays or plays that at least take place within the secular realm were turned into *autos sacramentales*. It was a matter of artistic and spiritual necessity that Calderón created many of these *autos* by means of de-individualizing and allegorizing his early dramas.

However much we are able to recognize the fundamentally Catholic nature of Calderón by examining his works, there is nevertheless something that is not so easy to define. It would be an oversimplification of Calderón's enormous body of work to explain it only as the consistent representation of a closed, specifically circumscribed world view. One can pass off small paradoxes if one accepts the somewhat vague definition of Calderón's work as a world in which "divine grace and human free will work together." *The Constant Prince*, for example, contains the following lines: "Every step . . . propels us toward that goal we're destined for. God is then insufficient to prevent that step being taken." While the significance of these words can be interpreted either in terms of the viewpoint of antiquity or of existentialism, the lines cannot be explained in terms of Christianity. And yet, though we know so little about his personality, it seems highly improbable that Calderón would have expressed such thought in conscious opposition to the prevailing doctrine of his own country and his age. It is more likely that we are dealing here with hyperboles that belong strictly to the sphere of the church but that were formulated in the above manner by Calderón because of dramatic necessity.

The cardinal question that Calderón puts to himself and that he answers within the context of his faith is that of the destination of mankind, the "why" of human life. The human being dressed in fur pelts, a situation that can be found at the beginning of many of his plays, is man who has been thrown out into the midst of nature. Like Calderón, such a man asks himself this very question. And he answers this question by binding himself to various orders: those of honor, the kingdom, and God. In *The Great World Theater*, the Master gives the final answer when he entitles the play that the people are about to perform before him "Do What Is Right!" Knowing how to do the right thing is a gift of grace, which in turn is a guarantee of salvation. For even "doing right" would have only limited meaning in a world that has been recognized as unreal were it not for the fact that belief in salvation cancels out "the fact that everything born is doomed to be the slave of its own natural bent" (Max Kommerell).

The most poetically beautiful image that Calderón offers to us as an expression of his religious views is doubtless that of his portrait of God as an artist, as a painter, as a singer, or—as in *The Great World Theater*—a theatrical director. The simple allegory of this work, in which human beings play-act under the direction of God and perform their roles either well or badly, says more about the interplay of divine will and human freedom than long theological tractates could be able to do.

The altar bread, which is handed out at the conclusion of all of Calderón's *autos sacramentales*, is not to be understood only as the reality of God in the sense of the Catholic belief. It is also a symbol of the redeemed world that has now become God's body. It is the threefold everything in the boldly baroque verbal interpretation of Calderón; God, bread, everything.

6. Calderón and Our Times

Recently, students have been warned against interpreting philosophies of an earlier day in a completely unhistorical fashion by approaching them from the perspective of modern world views. By sophistic means, one can do this at any time and with any philosophy.

Where theater is concerned, the matter of interpretation must be approached differently. The theater is not a historico-scientific institution but an establishment that must offer material of contemporary relevance. In public theaters, it would be futile to perform the works of a great dramatist as interpretations of his own age. Historically accurate productions are valid only on the stages of university theaters. Therefore, the director of a modern production of a great drama from a previous day shapes his direction according to the needs of his contemporaries.

These generalizations cannot be applied to Calderón's work. His basic attitudes toward life and toward the theater itself reveal so many decisive parallels to the prevailing views of our own age that the director offering a performance in a public theater need not think in these terms. His basically nonpsychological perspective, for example, is an attitude that seems to have determined the course of modern theater since Samuel Beckett. The human being dressed in fur pelts, man in his cave, symbolizes Calderón's belief that the human being must first realize himself. Thrown into a void, he must first affirm the reality of his own existence through his actions. The total dissolution of the space-time concept in Calderón's work—which not only signifies a creative poetic device but also functions as a conscious dramatic expression of the uncertainty of human life (which is perhaps only a dream) —corresponds to the relativity of modern drama whether we think of Pirandello or of Beckett.

This application to the Catholic dramatist Calderón of concepts from existentialism, atomic physics, and the theory of relativity, may seem at first sight to be oversophisticated. But this reproach can be refuted with the demonstrable fact that modern philosophy and modern science, after destroying the classical image of the physical world, returned to many of the presuppositions of pre-Renaissance times. Both disciplines reverted, namely, to the recognition of the total uncertainty of human life and therefore of its dependance upon suprahuman powers.

This, however, does not mean that the conclusions that modern man draws from this situation must lead to the same results as those reached by people three hundred and more years ago. The loss of modern man's anthropocentric world view has not necessarily resulted in a theocentric one. While in Calderón's work hopelessness is only seemingly so, leading directly and logically to the Catholic faith, in our time the feeling that there is no way out produces a multiplicity of new possibilities for modern man. It may be difficult for the contemporary reader to admit that Calderón's world view has meaning even without its specifically Catholic content. He may see Calderón as a dramatist who is comprehensible solely in terms of the Catholic spirit. He fails to consider, however, to what extent he has limited Calderón's effectiveness by making such a claim. We have long grown accustomed to recognizing the validity of the ancient world view of the Greek classicists for our own age, although it would not occur to anyone to believe in the existence of Greek gods. Similarly, it should be possible even for non-Catholics to accept the validity of Calderón's world view for our time.

Philosophy is, of course, intimately connected with the very essence of Calderón's drama. Ortega y Gasset has characterized the essence of the Spanish theater in a magnificent essay with the following words: "The possibilities for enjoyment contained in our Spanish theater belong to the sphere of Dionysus, just as do the mystical ecstasy of the monks and nuns of that age, those great individuals who abandoned themselves to ecstasy." The response to Spanish theater, Ortega says, "has nothing to do with being contemplative. Coolness is required for observation, distance between myself and the object. Whoever wants to look at a waterfall must above all take care that he is not carried along with it." Though this is certainly true, it is precisely my thesis that the intellectual played a decisive role in Calderón's drama that enables me to assert that Calderón's theater is very close to modern theater.

Aside from the fact that all theater is dionysian, and that contemplation only occurs in a later stage of sobriety, that is to say, after we have derived our pleasure from "being carried along" (this in spite of Brecht, whose plays offer such immediately effective theater that they give the lie to his own theories)— aside from this truism concerning theater, we must not overlook the fact that it is a Spaniard Ortega y Gasset who is evaluating Spanish theater, in other words, a Latin man who is evaluating a Latin phenomenon. The "triumph of the mind," to which Hugo Friedrich refers in connection with Calderón, is a basic demand of a Latin man on his art; for this art is itself first and foremost an artificial act. We know how carefully wrought Calderón's language is although it gives the impression of precipitant haste. Both the internal and external construction of his drama were also planned with great care. The confusing aspect of his work is not unlike that aspect that also confuses many contemporaries of Samuel Beckett, Jean Genet, and others. Calderón's logic is not synonymous with conventional school logic. He does not write in terms of casual connections. His heroes' experiences do not illustrate character development, for these figures are basically allegorical.

Whoever penetrates more deeply into Calderón's work will recognize that the wealth of his images is not the result of arbitrary choice. Rather, these images are clever contributions to the graduated intensity of the play as a whole. This dramaturgical and theatrical technique, peculiar not only to Calderón but also to the dramatists of his age in general, has made the survival of his work on the stage more difficult. The truths that modern drama have brought to light, however, provide a key to Calderón's work.

Let us keep in mind the parallels that exist between the baroque theater of illusion and our own theater of disillusion. Conscious theatricality in its own right was an aspect of baroque drama. Despite the presence of the most subtle technical devices, such theater was never designed to be an imitation of nature. Rather it represented at once both an expression of the dramatist's inner point of view and an aesthetic principle. As the technique of disillusion developed beyond the merely decorative into an integral part of the verbal substance of the plays in the theater of the absurd, Calderón's series of metaphors illustrate the continual transformation, indeed, the interchangeability of all graphically perceptible things.

Calderón's very significant use of the theatrical technique of illustration was first ascertained by Max Kommerell. His conclusion that Calderón's drama "represents a heightening of the ceremony of showing" results from his penetrating research into individual works. Indeed, Calderón made consistent and logical use of this technique, which was derived from the

Catholic mass. It is precisely because he does not bring real characters onto the stage, employing instead stock allegorical figures or—as Kommerell has perhaps somewhat too radically labeled his characters— "marionettes of God" that he is able to handle what are actually only symbols as he chooses. In doing this he remained within the context of baroque art in general. The essential figures in a baroque painting, for example, are always oriented toward the observer; the peripheral figures, like the observer himself, only function as mere spectators to the main action.

Like the masters of contemporary baroque painting, Calderón also knew how to involve his audience in the play's action in a twofold manner: as the observer of the action itself, and as witness to the action as seen through the eyes of the peripheral figures. This theater corresponds to the principles of modern dramaturgy and stands in opposition to naturalist theater in the following way: in the latter, the play transforms the spectator into a curious person who watches the play under the illusion that he is witness to a private occurrence; he believes he is being allowed to look through an invisible "fourth wall." Calderón's baroque theater as well as the theater of our own age is consciously presenting a performance for an audience.

To what extent these factors will be or even must be taken into consideration in modern productions of Calderón's works can only be answered in terms of the stage's actual requirements. Contemporary styles of production often oppose one another diametrically, oscillating between strictly intellectual stylization and luxuriant neobaroque spectacle. Since modern anti-psychological theater is only just beginning to establish itself as a formative stylistic influence, a new (or should we say, old) interpretation of Calderón's works can be seen at present only in some initial attempts.

7. Calderón's Legacy to World Theater

Calderón's works are baroque not only in form but also in their multiplicity. Whether his works are numbered at two hundred or—as some maintain—four hundred, this number is of little importance. The quantity of his works, which is extraordinary only in modern terms, was not at all unusual in Spain's golden age. As a matter of fact, Calderón was easily outdistanced by Lope de Vega as far as quantity goes. The Spanish dramatist of the sixteenth and seventeenth centuries was not a poet who had to plumb the depth of his soul with great struggle. Nor was he a restless experimentalist like Schiller, who often left brilliant work in fragments. Rather, he was a practical playwright who first of all had to understand his craft. That Calderón stood out qualitatively from the majority of his contemporaries was the mark of his genius; that he equaled them quantitatively was a matter of his practical expertise. It must not be overlooked, however, that Calderón, like almost all of his play-writing contemporaries, often appropriated other people's material, even entire acts of other plays, without reservation. For example, among his dramas are listed a *Celestina*, a *Faithful Shepherd*, even a *Don Quixote*. Other plays were, so to speak, collaborative works, in which only some of the acts were written by him. This was, of course, the common custom in other ages in which theater predominates.

It is difficult to divide Calderón's works into genres;

actually, it is an unnecessary task. Of course, one can broadly speak of comedies, dramas, festival plays, and religious works, if we wish to apply the labels of a later age to his works. Although we have little information on this subject, it is quite probable that Calderón began his career with plays in the style of Lope de Vega. This kind of play, called the cloak-and-sword play (*comedia de capa y espada*), was quite common at that time, the label itself having been derived from the two absolutely necessary stage properties of such works, the cloak and the sword. All of these plays are concerned above all with love and honor; they all sought to present variations on the basic elements of confusions, duels, and secret rendezvous, with untimely discoveries; and they all concluded with happy endings. These plays provided a cheerful likeness of life in Madrid in Calderón's day. As we know, Calderón participated in such affairs of love and honor when he himself was a young man. He himself poked fun at this genre when he wrote: "A brother or a father always arrives at the wrong time, and at such times there must always be a hidden lover and a veiled lady." Even during his own lifetime, people termed the various complications of cloak-and-sword plays "lances de Calderón" (Calderón's pranks).

The concept of honor, which in other contexts had quasi-religious significance, became a "code of gallantry" in social life. The form of this social life was itself theatrical. The serenades before grated windows, behind which listened a veiled lady, the affairs of honor between fathers and brothers of these ladies and their suitors—all of this was an amusing game, even when it deteriorated into a situation of deadly seriousness.

But even though the plays reflected one aspect of contemporary social life, we must keep in mind the fact that such plays represented a stylization of real occurrences that were adapted for the specific conditions of the stage. Thus such works corresponded with the fundamental concept of Mediterranean art that always placed a higher value on artifice than on realism. The public of Calderón's age had a predilection for the cloak-and-sword play. It was the fashion of the day, and no dramatist could ignore it since he was writing first and foremost for the theater as a living institution. It may have been in these years of writing the cloak-and-sword play that Calderón perfected his theatrical craft His first important play, for which he was recognized at the age of twenty-nine as one of Spain's most significant dramatists, was *The Phantom Lady*, whose technical subtlety and comic élan outshone even Lope de Vega's comedias.

The well of Calderón's comedias, usually estimated at one hundred and twenty, seemingly never runs dry. Even today hitherto obscure comedias by Calderón continue to crop up in the repertory of modern theaters, though no other comedia has yet attained the favored position of *The Phantom Lady*. Just to name a few of the most popular there are: *The Merchant of Women*; *The Loud Secret*, performed in eighteenth-century Italy in an adaptation by Carlo Gozzi; *The Ghostly Lover*, performed in France in 1659 and in Germany in 1669; *Tomorrow Is a New Day*; *The Game of Love and Fortune*, which became the basis for an opera libretto; *Beware of Still Waters*—considered to be Calderón's only comedia of character; *The Game of Hide-and-Seek*.

In 1637 the premiere of the drama *The Wonder-working Magician* gave proof of Calderón's enormous talent for the serious drama. Behind the passionate theatricality of this play, we can recognize Calderón's consistent basic philosophy. The best of these serious dramas are: *The Devotion to the Cross, Life Is a Dream, The Constant Prince, Jealousy, The Greatest Monster, The Surgeon of His Honor, The Schism in England, In This Life Everything Is True and Everything Is False, The Daughter of Air, Poisoned and Cured, The Mayor of Zalamea, Absalom's Locks, The Grand Duke of Gandia.*

Jealousy, The Greatest Monster is one of the earliest dramatic adaptations of the story of Herod and Mariamne. Because of its "accursed dagger," this drama, at least superficially, was the prototype of the German drama of fate. *The Surgeon of His Honor* was translated into seven foreign languages within a short time after its Spanish premiere. Like *The Painter of His Dishonor*, it harshly offered the theatergoer the ultimate tragic consequences of dedication to honor being carried too far. In *The Schism in England*, Calderón, handling a subject of contemporary importance, dramatized the defection of Henry VIII from the Church of Rome. *In This Life Everything Is True and Everything Is False* is a variation on the theme of *Life Is a Dream.*

Only one of Calderón's festival plays, which were chiefly written for the garden theater of Buen Retiro, has survived on the stages of European theater: *Love, The Greatest Enchantment.*

August Wilhelm Schlegel claims that Calderón's most characteristic works are the *autos sacramentales,* the approximately eighty religious one-act plays that were offered to the public during the feast of Corpus Christi. In their own day, these *autos* served above all to make theatrically visual the controversial dogma of the eucharist. That these plays possessed authentic power above and beyond this specifically religious context is proved by the fact that they continued to be good theater in Spain into the eighteenth century and were revived in the nineteenth and twentieth centuries. For the allegories of these plays, as embodied by their characters, represent not disguises but revelations. Through these allegorical figures Calderón's symbolic language is conveyed more clearly and more directly than through the persons and plots of any of his other works. The visualization of spiritual concepts never appears more distinctly than in these works.

Calderón found the subjects for these *autos* both in mythology and in the Bible. He also liked to transform his own earlier plays into *autos*, allowing his earlier characters to become allegories. *The Surgeon of His Honor*, *Life Is a Dream*, and even *Love, The Greatest Enchantment* were all transmuted into *autos*. Besides *The Great World Theater*, contemporary theater includes in its repertory such *autos* as *Belshazzar's Feast*, and *The Mysteries of the Sacred Mass*. *Divine Orpheus*, which is perhaps Calderón's finest *auto*, has yet to be rescued by a modern producer. This work, in which God creates the world through song, is considered by Hugo Friedrich to represent "the last happy hour of the ancient and now concluding marriage between Christianity and classical antiquity, between poetry and faith."

In addition to his comedias and *autos*, Calderón

wrote approximately twenty interludes and other short plays.

Understandably, productions in the style intended by Calderón were only possible in Spain and even there only so long as the spirit of the golden age still prevailed. With the political decline of Spain, which led to the insignificance of this state in European power politics, the baroque, the style of Calderón's theater, disappeared from the Iberian peninsula. Later Spanish drama is characterized by a complete turning away from baroque drama and by the emergence of new forms. If one tries to conjure up Calderón's bygone and more or less inaccessible world, the age-old skepticism concerning a revival of his works becomes comprehensible. His influence on the younger dramatists of his age was strong. But, although Spanish drama was still feasting on Calderón even into the eighteenth century, the name of only one of his successors, Agustín Moreto, is known today in the world of the theater.

In Spain the nineteenth century seemed to be marked by a strange lack of comprehension of Calderón. While he was honored on the occasion of the bicentennial of his death with elaborate celebrations, processions, and royal banquets, he was praised either as the patriot or the Catholic or by others as the "anti-absolutist" writer of *The Mayor of Zalamea*. Today the number of his works in the repertory of Spanish theater is relatively small.

Calderón exerted a substantial influence on French, Italian, and English poets and dramatists. Just as he himself had unhesitatingly borrowed material, so, too, did later dramatists make use of his themes: in France there were, for example, Thomas Corneille, Philippe Quinault, Paul Scarron, and Alain-René Lesage; in Italy, Carlo Gozzi; and in England, John Dryden. Pierre Corneille's *Héraclius* has its model in Calderón's *In This Life Everything Is True and Everything Is False*. Molière's *The Learned Women* arises in part from *You Can't Play with Love*. The third act of Beaumarchais's *The Marriage of Figaro* is derived from Calderón's *A House with Two Entrances Is Hard to Protect*. Several of Calderón's plays were translated by Percy Bysshe Shelley, who is said to have read them "with enormous astonishment and delight." That Calderón's plays have seldom been performed on the stages of France, Italy, and England can perhaps be explained by the prevailing tendency in these countries, even today, to perform only the works of their own dramatists.

In Germany, Calderón's works were frequently played in free translations by itinerant actors as early as the seventeenth century. In the eighteenth century, these works still lived in many repertories. *Life Is a Dream* was performed in Munich in 1666, while Calderón was still alive. In 1674, *The Jealousy of Herod* was performed in Dresden. The most important German troupe of the seventeenth century, that of Master Johannes Velten, performed among other works by Calderón, *The Daughter of Air, Jealousy, The Greatest Monster*, and *Life Is a Dream*. Although what these itinerant troupes performed conveyed little of Calderón's style or of his ideas, they did present the content of his plays. And it was precisely because this content appeared in such a distorted form that these plays have proved they possess a theatricality whose effectiveness cannot be weakened by anything.

Gotthold Lessing and Goethe both attempted to establish Calderón in their theaters, each of which became an institution for the dissemination of higher culture. It is significant that such attempts were resisted by some and hailed with praise by others. Lessing wanted to translate *The Mayor of Zalamea* himself. A sizable compendium of Goethe's praises of Calderón could easily be made, but neither his interest in Calderón nor his actual attempts to revive Calderón on the stage had any lasting success. Goethe's opinions impress us as being strikingly modern. Indeed, they established at that time a new conception of Calderón's work, which is only beginning to gain ground in recent decades. Above all, Goethe recognized the primary intention of Calderón when he wrote: "I feel confident that I could greatly delight both cultured and lower classes alike by performing Calderón's works, assuming the necessary changes are made, at any county fair, even on a stage made of planks supported by barrels."

Goethe also stressed the influence of Calderón's theater on world theater when he described his plays as reflecting the "quintessence of humanity." By recognizing the primacy of the intellectual in Calderón's work, Goethe was also the first to contradict the prevailing opinion that Calderón was both pompous and excessively emotional. Goethe seems almost to approach a definition of our modern theater when he asserted about *The Daughter of Air*: "What is to be said about this play can be said about all the plays of this dramatist. He does not imbue his works with a real observation of nature; rather, he is totally theatrical, histrionic. There is not a trace of what we call illusion, particularly of that type that produces emotion. His design is clearly apprehensible by the reason." As a poet, Goethe tried to translate Calderón's fragmentary *A Tragic Play in the Christian World*. As a theatrical director, he staged *Life Is a Dream*, *Zenobia*, and *The Constant Prince*, which he particularly liked.

Because of the liking of both Goethe and the German Romantic poets for Calderón's works, the first German productions that can be taken seriously in a literary way were offered during the second half of the eighteenth century. In later years, the German theater continued to make attempts to establish Calderón on the stage, as the theater of no other country did, despite the stubborn resistance of many theater people and the often very cool reception of audiences. The style of these performances was, to be sure, hardly different from the style in which other plays were staged in the nineteenth century. This method did little to contribute to a better understanding of Calderón's work.

The German attempt, as well as the French, to produce Calderón's works as part of the Catholic revival at the beginning of the twentieth century failed because of the insufficient skill of those involved.

Thus it is to the credit of a few individuals to have recognized Calderón's modernity and to have proved it to some extent. In this connection it is important to point to the rather paradoxical fact that the rediscovery of Calderón—for we can really speak of a rediscovery since the middle of our century—came about through the efforts of non-Catholics. As early as the 1920s, the German novelist and dramatist Lion Feuchtwanger pointed the way to Calderón's work. For Feuchtwanger saw in the Catholicism of this dramatist only *one* realization of a grand cosmic order. In our own age, it was especially Albert Camus and Giorgio Strehler who, inspired by Calderón's brilliant theatricality, evaluated his Catholic point of view as a grandiose example of a cosmic world image. The fact that John Arden, a dramatist in his own right and anything but a philologically oriented translator, has rendered Calderón's plays into English proves once again that there is general recognition of Calderón's modernity.

A new image of Calderón seems to be in the process of establishing itself in some parts of Europe, perhaps because in these other countries it is not necessary, as it is in Germany, to first throw overboard the ballast of an old stage tradition. It is indeed quite possible that works that have been forgotten or that have been held in less high regard will be recalled to life tomorrow or the next day by means of new translations or new productions.

Only those plays that already belong to the vital tradition of European theater will be examined in the following pages. Each discussion contains information about historical and modern productions in Europe and America.

PLAYS

The Phantom Lady

Calderón's most frequently performed comedia was probably written in 1629. The very first scene reveals Calderón's skillful dramatic technique —it manages with a few strokes to create the atmosphere of contemporary cloak-and-sword plays. A veiled lady, Doña Angela, comes running through the wings onto the stage; she begs an unknown cavalier, Don Manuel, for protection against an anonymous pursuer. The servant Cosme's attempt to prevent the pursuit by delaying tactics gives rise to the play's first duel. Don Manuel is slightly wounded. Don Juan appears just in time to settle the conflict. It is now revealed that Don Manuel, an old friend of Don Juan, is to be his house guest during his stay in Madrid, and that the pursuer is Don Juan's brother, Don Luis. What is not revealed is that the veiled lady is the sister who, being kept in strict seclusion by her brothers because she is a widow, has slipped out of the house to watch the festivities.

In the second scene we learn—and would not expect otherwise—that the lady of the house, Angela, has fallen in love with Don Manuel. She finds out that Don Manuel has been lodged in the room next to hers. A secret door, which in the guest room is concealed by a glass cabinet, leads from one room to the other.

The concealed door is a popular dramatic cliché. Calderón employed this device in other plays as well, even in his serious ones. Indeed, the painted cliffs in the set of *Apollo and Clymene*, which camouflage the entrance to a cave, are to be understood as just such a secret door. I shall not venture to say whether or not the secret door in *The Phantom Lady* represents some kind of deeper symbolism. To be sure, a particularly enthusiastic Calderón interpreter has maintained that the glass cabinet embodies the deceptiveness of everything that is perceptible to the senses.

When Manuel and his servant Cosme (one of the numerous gracioso characters in Calderón's comedias) leave the guest room, Angela and her maid enter it through the secret door. Both of them rummage through the stranger's belongings. Before they leave Angela leaves behind a little note. Cosme returns, is alarmed at the disorder he finds, and fears that a ghost has wreaked the havoc he sees.

Now the plot unfolds through complicated actions that mystify the male characters. A secret exchange of letters between Angela and Manuel begins. But neither Manuel nor Cosme know that Angela lives in the house. In one scene, carrying a basket of linen into Manuel's room, Cosme enters with a lit candle. A very comical scene develops at this point: Cosme is still afraid of the supposed ghost whom he does not see, since Angela always manages to place herself behind his back and thus conceal herself from him. When she blows out the candle, Cosme becomes paralyzed with fear. During her next visit, Angela is surprised by Manuel himself. She claims to be a supernatural being, but Manuel challenges this by threatening her with a sword. She once again flees from the room. The play becomes more intense in the following scene, in which Angela leads Don Manuel blindfolded into her room by means of the secret door. There, magnificently served by her maids, Angela herself receives him, splendidly dressed. Don Manuel feels himself to be in seventh heaven. But this idyll is destroyed by the arrival of one of Angela's brothers. Manuel is quickly returned to his own room.

A short time later, Manuel is brought back once again by Angela's maid. Because it is dark, she takes Cosme's hand by mistake instead of that of his master. In this manner, Cosme, too, is allowed into the lady's room, and the earlier scene is repeated in a parodistic form. This time the scene is interrupted by Angela's other brother. In the ensuing confusion, Cosme escapes back into his master's room. The brother pursues him through the secret door that Cosme has left open, believing that Manuel has insulted his sister's honor. It almost comes to a fatal duel. But cleverly arranged concluding events resolve the conflict so that the play ends happily.

We must constantly bear in mind that this play from a strange age and a strange country, which enchants us precisely by virtue of its exoticism, was received by the Spanish public of Calderón's day in a totally different manner. What strikes us as being exotic was for the Spaniards a matter of everyday occurrence. This comedia offered the large masses of the lower classes a glimpse of life in higher society and satisfaction of a curiosity that exists in all ages. A similar curiosity is satisfied today in those films about wealthy people living in beautiful homes. One cannot speak here of social criticism. Those aspects of Calderón's plays that seem to us today to be parodistic (and which are often consciously interpreted as such by modern directors) struck Calderón's own public as mere situation comedy. In Calderón's time, cloak-and-sword plays were absolutely run-of-the-mill, mere light entertainment. That despite this, some of these plays, particularly his *Phantom Lady*, have remained timeless contributions to the repertory of theater, speaks for the special genius of their author, Calderón.

After the premiere of *The Phantom Lady* in Madrid in November 1629, this play was performed in Paris in 1641. In 1664 it was performed in England, in 1670 in Holland, both times in translations of the French version. The first German performance took place in 1721 in Hamburg. Its title can be translated as: *Spirito Folletto, the Ghost of Isabella Who Pursues Her Faithless Lover in Nineteen Appearances, also with Harlequin, a Passenger Who Is also Tormented by Spirits Everywhere*. In 1741 the play appeared again in Frankfurt under a title that can be translated as *Spirito Foletto, or Angiola, the Amorous Ghost*. During the remainder of the eighteenth century and the nineteenth century, this play was frequently performed in Munich, Frankfurt, Dresden, and Vienna.

In 1920 Max Reinhardt produced *The Phantom Lady* in its most important poetic translation, that of Hugo von Hofmannsthal. In 1940 it was produced by Erich Engel in the Deutsches Theater, Berlin. This production, which was in itself excellent, nevertheless suffered from the same misconception that harms so many productions of Calderón's works, that is, that such productions attempt to surmount Calderón's own strict dramatic form by aiming for a comedy of character in the manner of Shakespeare. In this way, however, the characters become unnecessarily encumbered and lose their lightness, which must after all be an intrinsic part of their nature because they are meant to be only a poetic expression of concepts. If, in addition to this, the director gives too free a rein to the individuality of great actors, as Engel is said to have done, the performance is contrary to the dramatist's intentions.

Erich Fritz Brücklmeier's production of *The Phantom Lady* in Düsseldorf in 1956 was primarily conceived as a presentation of a specifically Spanish play. The stage sets employed motifs derived from Miró and Picasso, and Spanish love songs were part of the musical score. The staging was stylistically close to that of *commedia dell'arte*.

Günther Lüders staged *The Phantom Lady* at the Cuvilliéstheater in Munich on 28 October 1958. His production was very discreet, "not parodistic, only somewhat ironic—this seemed quite necessary as a means of bringing temporal distance." Elfriede Kuzmany played Angela more as the loving woman than the ghost, a performance that led one critic to observe that this interpretation lacked Spanish pepper. This production seems to have suffered from the same misconception as did that of Engel. Elfriede Kuzmany interpreted her role as if the play were a comedy of character. But, as K. H. Ruppel wrote, "Calderón's figures do not create form, they merely illuminate it."

In 1965 the Institute for Advanced Studies in the

Life Is a Dream, a profound theatrical presentation of the nature of reality and illusion, is by general consent considered one of the masterpieces of world drama. Segismundo is a character of limitless interpretative possibilities. Here is the Segismundo (as played by Stephen Joyce) who kills and tries to rape after his first release from the tower in which he has been sequestered from birth. Photograph from the Yale Repertory Theater production in March 1972.

The Mayor of Zalamea centers on the rape of Isabel by
the arrogant officer Don Álvaro. Here the dishonored
Isabel, cast aside in the forest after Don Álvaro has satisfied his lust, finds her father, Crespo, who had been tied
up by Álvaro's men to prevent him from rescuing her. In
Ulrich Erfurth's staging of this play (photograph above),
offered in 1961 in Hamburg, the sensuality is emphasized.
Crespo was presented in this production as a "self-sufficient, peasantlike patriarch."
ROSEMARIE CLAUSEN, HAMBURG

Calderón is said to have been a common soldier for many years before he became an officer. This experience was so much a part of him that he offered in *The Mayor of Zalamea* an unforgettable picture of the total wretchedness of the military life. The camp follower is never far from the military, but the theater has few characterizations of such a woman to equal that of Calderón's La Chispa (center). Photograph from Rudolf Sellner's production at the Berlin Schillertheater in 1961.

JLSE BUHS, BERLIN

Comic relief in the Spanish comedia was often provided
by the cavalier-servant pair, in the Don Quixote–Sancho
Panza tradition. Three centuries have not dimmed the
delights of the superb dialogue between Don Mendo, the
lovestruck, foolish, impoverished squire, and his faithful,
hungry, down-to-earth servant Nuño, which Calderón
offered in *The Mayor of Zalamea*. Photograph from
Rudolf Sellner's production at the Berlin Schillertheater
in 1961.

JLSE BUHS, BERLIN

Calderón wrote *The Great World Theater* when he was
seventy-five years old. A religious-allegorical play, it re-
flects Calderón's deepest vision of life, though completely
subsumed into theatrical art of the highest kind. In a
flight of baroque imagination Calderón casts God (the
Master) as a theatrical director and dramatist and turns
life into a stage. Above, the Master delivers his verdict to
the "actors" who have fretted away their hour on the
stage. Since 1924 this play has been presented outdoors in
front of the Church of the Pilgrims in Einsiedeln, Switzerland (photograph above).

SWISS NATIONAL TOURIST OFFICE

Love, The Greatest Enchantment is said to be the most perfect baroque play of the golden age of Spain. Poetry, splendor, magic, love, dance, elaborate stage effects, contributed to making this immortal story of Circe and Ulysses a masterpiece of total theater. Here Ulysses's startled crew, with Ulysses at the center, are confronted by a pack of wild animals who urge them with human gestures to sail on. Photograph from Heinrich Koch's production at the Deutsches Schauspielhaus in Hamburg, 1955.

About *The Constant Prince*, Goethe wrote: "What a play! . . . In this single work the great Catholic poet has hoisted himself into a sphere that has not even been reached by Shakespeare. No production of any work either before or since Calderón's day has even been remotely able to approach this tragedy." In the scene above the starving Fernando still defies the will of the king of Fez. The Moor Muley (center), torn between his duty to the king and his friendship with Fernando, looks on. Photograph from the Munich Kammerspiel production, 1953.

The home of the Spanish comedia for many years were the courtyards (*corrales*) of hospitals. Thus, one of the great theater periods in the western world flourished in the modest setting of an open-air stage surrounded by the walls of buildings. Dramas of unsurpassed greatness were presented by itinerant troupes on stages that were hastily constructed and dismantled as the need arose. In Ciudad Real the restored *corral* of Almagro (see above) offers productions in the golden-age style.

SPANISH NATIONAL TOURIST OFFICE

Theatre Arts (IASTA) presented a workshop production of *The Phantom Lady*, in a translation by Edwin Honig, at the Library of Congress in Washington, D.C. José Luis Alonso, who heads the Teatro Nacional Maria Guerrero in Madrid, directed. Sets and costumes were by Francisco Nieva of Madrid. So that the production would have authentic detail, accessories and numerous properties were obtained from Spain.

Time and again people have tried to use *The Phantom Lady* as the basis of an opera libretto. But even the most recent attempts to set this work to music, those by Weingartner and Wimberger, gave rise to an unanimous critical opinion: Calderón on his own is better.

The Wonder-working Magician

In 1794, Goethe wrote the following opinion of this work that was supposedly written as early as 1631: "The wonderful magician presents the subject of Doctor Faustus on an unbelievably grand scale." That this work nevertheless was hardly able to establish itself on the European stage because it was so greatly outshone by Goethe's own *Faust* can be explained by totally different attitudes harbored by later generations of theatergoers. Max Kommerell correctly designates Calderón as that dramatist who truly fulfilled to its potential the Middle Ages, a Middle Ages whose theatrical criterion was that of graphic representation of intellectual and spiritual problems. Modern theater wrongly believed that this was a vulgarization of theater and sought its own ideal in the poetic spiritualization of the plot, such as was achieved by Goethe in his *Iphigenia* or *Tasso*. The modern spectator was no longer able to absorb, and is perhaps still unable to absorb, intellectual content that is presented through the medium of an image or a theatrical effect.

Kommerell called Calderón the dramatist who brought the theater of the Middle Ages to fruition primarily for the reason that he was the first to provide the medieval play with a poetically authentic language. This language was not first and foremost a medium through which abstract ideas could be imparted. Rather, because of its baroque "beauty," this language became a factor that contributed to and determined the theatrical effectiveness of Calderón's plays. Only by keeping this different point of view in mind, are we able to realize that such plays as *The Wonder-working Magician* are indeed highly philosophical works, not childlike theater. Only the means by which this philosophy is expressed are still unusual. But these means are more appropriate to the theater than those theatrical means that have been employed in the eighteenth, nineteenth, and, for the most part, the twentieth century.

The model that Calderón probably used for this play was the comedia, *The Demon's Slave*, written by Antonio Mira de Amescua. There is also an extant work by Guillén de Castro y Bellvis on this theme. The content in the play was contained in the legend concerning Saint Cyprian and Saint Justina, both of whom suffered martyrdom in the fourth century. Cyprian is said to have been a fanatical opponent of Christianity before his baptism.

As a great and joyful festival is taking place in Antioch to celebrate the construction of a temple for the worship of Jupiter, the scholar Cipriano withdraws with his books into a lonely mountainous region. He sends his servants, the play's graciosos, into the city. Alone, he encounters the Demon who has disguised himself as a merchant. A philosophical conversation between the two gradually evolves. Cipriano cannot believe that each of the various gods has different things to say: "And though he may split into one, or two, or several persons, the deity in essence must be one." If God is omniscient, yet promises victory to two parties when only one side can really win, how can he be said to be all good? This chain of thoughts must lead in Calderón's works to monotheism, that is, to Christianity, even if his Cipriano at first only admits this concept hypothetically:

> "There be a God?
> Most all-loving, most all-merciful,
> Omnipotent and omniscient?
> . . . .
> Primal beginning, yet without beginning,
> A being begotten by himself,
> A single power, a single will.
> . . . .
> One godhead quite unbounded
> Must be essence undivided,
> Of all causes first the cause."

Naturally, Calderón employs both in his dialogue and in his concluding hypotheses those forms and expressions that were customary in contemporary academic disputation. These passages nevertheless have a philosophical significance and logical consistency beyond any denominational tendency.

The Demon breaks the conversation off, because strangers approach. Now follows once again a theatrically adroit scene, for the philosophical conversation must be quickly interrupted by dramatic action. Theater demands its primary rights. The youths Lelio and Florio enter, in order to engage in a duel for the sake of the beautiful Justina, whom they both love. Cipriano separates the combatants and promises to propose both their suits to Justina for them.

The Christian girl, Justina, whose birth and origins are shrouded in mystery, lives with her foster father Lisandro, also a Christian. When Lisandro is forced to flee from his house because of an action brought against him for debt, Cipriano makes use of this opportunity to call upon Justina. But the Demon has already bewitched him. Without wanting to, Cipriano himself succumbs to the girl's beauty. When she refuses the offers of both of the two youths, he dares to court her in his own name. Justina is alarmed and asks him to leave her.

The next scene is once again such pure theater that even a cloak-and-sword comedia could not be more entertaining. The Demon, who also seeks to possess Justina's soul, lets himself down on a rope from Justina's balcony just as Lelio and Florio approach her house, each from a different side. Each of the youths now believes that the man on the rope is his rival. A new duel ensues. Once again the duelers are separated by Cipriano. The two then angrily give up their suit. Cipriano once again asks for Justina's hand but is once again rebuffed. Then he appeals to hell for help and promises to give up his soul as the price for Justina's favor.

This time the Demon appears before Cipriano amid fearful theatrical thunder and identifies himself in his true form. In order to win Justina, the Demon plays the same game once again before Lelio; once again he leaves her house as if he were her lover. This time, however, Lelio realizes that the man on the rope is not Florio. The result is that the two rejected suitors insult the unsuspecting Justina by calling her a hypocrite. Since she is unable to counter their reproaches and defend herself with convincing argument, even her foster father Lisandro begins to have doubts in her. The latter has just returned with the terrible announcement that the emperor Decius has ordered the governor of the city to murder all its Christian inhabitants.

In order to gain Justina's love, Cipriano wants to learn the art of magic from the Demon. Therefore, he signs a pact with his own blood. In full possession of magical powers, he now feels himself to be superior even to the Demon. The Demon, however, knowing that Justina's love is necessary, sneaks into her room in order to turn her head with all sorts of tricks. This scene is considered to be one of the most masterful in all of Calderón's works. Unlike those saints in medieval paintings, this Justina is not pursued by voluptuous and caricatured masks. Instead, invisible choruses sing songs to her about the beauties of nature. They could just as well have rendered her inner mood, alluding to her unconscious love for Cipriano. Only her Christian convictions prevent her union with him. Her monologue, after she has heard the seductive voices, is a poem of great beauty. She believes that she has heard the answers to her questions in the songs of the nightingale, the grape, and the flower, that is to say, through the forces of nature that are seeking to persuade her of the necessity of love. Finally, she admits to herself the secret love that she feels for Cipriano. At this moment, the Demon, who wishes to lead her to Cipriano, appears.

Cipriano's presence strengthens Justina's resistance. Indeed, torment and passion could have vanquished her spirit, but her will is stronger than her emotions. She says openly: "I am powerless in my thought, but my act is in my power." In the middle of a passionate dialogue, that is to say, by means of genuine theater, Calderón dramatically unfolds before us the whole problematic nature of human free will, a problem he as well as his contemporaries were deeply preoccupied with. The human being can dominate his actions by his thought. The Demon has no power in opposition to the freedom of thought, at least, of rational thought. In other words, he has no power against a rational decision made by the free will. For the play asserts: "Were the will ever free, if it would bow to compulsion?"

When the Demon finally attempts to abduct Justina by force, she appeals to God. Finding herself alone once again, she does not know whether the Demon is a phantom of her fear or whether he exists in reality.

Cipriano finally succeeds in magically conjuring up a vision of Justina. But just as he is about to lift her veil, believing that he is embracing the real Justina, he sees a corpse before him. The vision disappears with the tendentious assertion characteristic not only of Calderón but of his whole age: "Cipriano, such are all the glories of the world you so covet." Now Cipriano demands the return of his soul from the Demon, since the Demon has not lived up to his part of the bargain. A quarrel ensues between the two. The Demon makes evasions; Cipriano attacks him with his sword, but the Demon is stronger and can surely kill him. At this point, Cipriano appeals to the God of the Christians and is freed from his pact.

Justina and her foster father are taken prisoner by the governor. Justina is condemned to death. Cipriano then appears as a penitent and publicly acknowledges Christ. Alone with Justina, he reveals to her the transformation that has taken place in his heart. He does not believe that God can forgive him until Justina describes the unlimited compassion of the Christian God. The two are led to their execution together, Cipriano in the certainty of his new faith, Justina pervaded with joy because she has been united with Cipriano in a higher form of love. At the end, a violent storm springs up. A curtain rises at the rear of the stage where one sees a scaffold with the beheaded bodies of Justina and Cipriano. Over the scaffold, in the air, sitting on a winged serpent, is the Demon. God's will compels the Demon to publicly reveal the truth. This final triumph of the divine will over the demonic, made visual through a powerful theatrical appearance, provides the solution to the play's spiritual and intellectual problems.

As a complement to the main plot, Calderón has also woven into the play a number of scenes in which the comical servants appear, both of whom love Justina's maid. But in contrast to the solution of the conflict that unites the pair Cipriano and Justina, the maid's solution is very realistic: she concludes a compromise whereby each of the two servants is to be her lover on alternate days.

The claims that many scholars have made concerning the parallels between *The Wonder-working Magician* and Goethe's *Faust* cannot really be supported by fact. For example, the scholar Joseph Gregor's comparison of Justina's instinctive loathing for the Demon, which leads to her salvation, with Gretchen's distrust of Mephistopheles is perhaps psychologically interesting. There is, however, hardly any connection between the two scenes in which these feelings are presented. On the other hand, Max Kommerell is right in asserting that it is precisely in this play that the medieval concept of man, which regarded him as an object standing between divine and demonic influences, can be seen as opposed to Goethe's psychological concept of man who has to decide between reason and instinct. Apart from the fact that the medieval form was theatrically more effective, since it was able to make suprahuman powers graphic, Calderón would not have been able to portray the victory of reason (that is to say, of the will) so convincingly had the will merely signified an emotional phenomenon devoid of its metaphysical orientation.

The premiere of *The Wonder-working Magician* took place in 1637.

In 1947, director Giorgio Strehler discovered this play and staged it in his Piccolo Teatro in Milan. This is said to have been the first Italian performance of this play. In 1960, in connection with the Eucharistic Congress, which was held in Munich that year, a production of *The Wonder-working Magician* was put on at the Residenztheater there. This production, which is the only well-known German staging of this work in our day, failed because its director lacked knowledge of the real Calderón. Mere arabesques were performed: the basic content and fundamental meaning of the play were hardly hinted at. It was a piece of baroque stucco, which failed to project the architectonic construction of the play.

The Devotion to the Cross

It is generally assumed that this three-act drama was written in the year 1634. The source of the plot is unknown, though it probably stems from one of the numerous legends of the cross in which the cross itself possesses the character of a talisman. In Calderón's play, this legend is utilized to glorify the Catholic belief in miracles. This play is also the most controversial of Calderón's works. Some critics recognize the presence of both fetishism and paganism in this drama, while others view it as a drama of fate. Only romantic spirits, in the best sense of the word, for example, E. T. A. Hoffmann, were able to see the particular poetic beauty of this work as well as its grandiose theatricality.

After an introductory scene involving a pair of graciosos, this drama begins with the obligatory duel, which was an almost routine form of exposition. Lisardo is engaged in combat with Eusebio, who is courting Julia, Lisardo's sister, without having bothered to obtain her father's consent. According to the Spanish concept of honor, this was sufficient cause for the son of the family to defend his family's honor with the sword. Moreover, Eusebio's origins are unknown. He is one of the Calderón heroes who as infants were found by shepherds in isolated regions. Not only had he been found at the foot of a cross but he also had the sign of the cross on his chest. He had also been preserved from danger many times in his life in a more or less magical way by a cross. He fatally wounds Lisardo. Honor demands that the victor make it possible for the dying loser to make his last confession. Eusebio carries Lisardo to a hermit. Meanwhile, Julia's father, who has heard of Eusebio's courting, has ordered her to enter a convent.

Eusebio tries to persuade Julia to flee with him. But once again—and in the manner of a cloak-and-sword drama—the father arrives at the wrong time and Julia must hide Eusebio. The father now reveals a secret to his daughter. Because he had once doubted his wife's faithfulness, he had led her to a lonely region just before she was due to give birth to her child. He is prevented from continuing his report since the body of his son Lisardo is brought in at this moment. This dramatic device that heightens the play's tension is a favorite one of Calderón. Indeed, such exciting techniques of suspense are also to be seen in the first conversation between the Demon and Cipriano in *The Wonder-working Magician*.

Deeply enraged at Eusebio, the father has his daughter locked in her room. When Eusebio comes out of his hiding place, Julia showers him with reproaches. She nevertheless helps him to escape though she wishes never to see him again.

The second act provides a real uproar. Eusebio has become the captain of a band of robbers. He and his band of thieves attack peasants as well as rich people. He is motivated simply by the personal despair caused by an unjust fate: his is a kind of revenge arising out of world-weariness. Or, it can be seen as the activity of human free will that stands diametrically opposed to God's grace.

Eusebio attacks the priest Alberto as the latter is on a journey. The bullet that was to hit him lodges itself in a book that the priest is wearing on his chest. The book contains a report concerning the miracle of the cross. Eusebio, deeply gripped by these events, allows Alberto to continue on his way.

In the meantime, Julia's father and a crowd of peasants approach. He now continues the story about the casting out of his wife. At that time, he had been prepared to kill her. She clung fast to a cross that she called upon as a witness of her innocence. Although he had already begun to have misgivings about his suspicion, he stabbed her and fled home. Through the miracle of the cross, he found her alive the next morning and in his room: in her arms was the new-born Julia, who had the sign of the cross on her chest as a mark of the miracle. His happiness would have been complete if his wife had not spoken of a twin, whom she had had to leave behind at the foot of the cross. Once again, the monologue is interrupted at its most exciting point, by the servant's announcement that the robbers are approaching.

Driven by frustrated passion, Eusebio, who in the meantime has been secretly married to Julia, steals into the convent, meaning to possess Julia on any terms. But when he discovers the presence of the sign of the cross on her breast, he changes his mind and flees. Julia is thrown into despair at his rejection and follows him. But when she reaches the foot of the convent's walls, she is seized by repentance and seeks to return. Now, however, the ladder that she had used for her escape has been carried away. Her return to the cloister is impossible. She believes that she must recognize this act as a definite denial of divine grace. In her desperation she now decides, like Eusebio, to plunge herself into sin.

Disguised as a robber, she meets Eusebio and his band. (This convention, that of a woman dressed in men's clothing, was very popular in Spanish theater.) Keeping her face concealed, she challenges her husband to a duel but he refuses. She then reveals her identity to Eusebio and recounts her flight from the convent and the way she had obtained men's clothing by murdering innocent people. Eusebio pleads with her in vain to return to the convent.

A new fight with the people of Julia's father ensues, and the robbers are dispersed. Julia tries to gather them together once again. Eusebio and his father-in-law meet, but an undefined feeling prevents both of them from fighting. The arriving peasants force Eusebio to flee. He falls from a high cliff and is mortally wounded. At the foot of the cross, where the father once upon a time banished his wife, he now finds the dying Eusebio. He recognizes that he is the lost son by the sign of the cross on his chest. Eusebio begs forgiveness. Julia, too, confesses her guilt to her father, but when he attempts to murder her as punishment for her sins, she embraces the cross in great fear, as her mother had done. As she does this, the cross is carried aloft, and she disappears with it into the air.

One must keep in mind the theatrical grandeur of the plot's construction, despite the absurdity of many of the play's situations. Dramatic theory has been totally converted into action. The initial duel and the suspenseful buildup of the exposition, achieved by means of the father's interrupted narration, is followed by the second act's robber romanticism and the adventurous escape from the convent. In the third act, Calderón offers wildly changing pictures of battle until the touching and miraculous recognition scenes bring the play's action to a conclusion. The powerful scene, which does not give the impression of having been merely tagged on, ends the drama on a high note. Throughout runs the vein of the delightful jokes of the graciosos.

The cross as a visible symbol of grace prevails over the false decision of the individual will. The passion of love, even if it goes astray, is purified by the cross and raised above its earthly imperfection. The frequently criticized immorality of the play is negated by its higher form of religiosity. In no other of Calderón's plays can we so directly experience the faith of his age, the core of which was divine grace or the visible intervention of a higher power in human life. Salvation is not the calculable reward for having lived a moral life; in other words, it cannot be determined by man himself. The Portuguese saying that "God writes straight even on crooked lines," which Paul Claudel used as the motto of his play *The Silken Slipper*, had already been given dramatic form in *The Devotion to the Cross*.

It is false to speak here of a fate drama in the narrower sense of the term, because the sign of the cross is not just some sort of fetish for a Christian writer; it is, rather, always a sign of the possibility of grace. The point here is the ability of Christian grace to break through and alter a destiny created by fateful familial relationships.

That *The Devotion to the Cross* is frequently compared to *Romeo and Juliet* is to be expected. But it is precisely through such a comparison that the essential difference in the world view of Calderón and Shakespeare becomes clear. Shakespeare's drama is anthropocentric and must logically end in tragedy; Calderón's drama represents a theocentric point of view, according to which even the most confused of destinies can be resolved and fulfilled in a higher sense.

Calderón's dramatic genius can also be seen in the fact that he was able to combine in a most original manner a wealth of traditional motifs—incestuous love, parental prohibition of marriage, the good man turned robber out of despair, the woman disguised as a man—and yet create from all of these a unified plot.

The premiere of *The Devotion to the Cross* took place in 1643. In Germany the play was first presented by the Holbein Society in Bamberg in 1811, directed by E. T. A. Hoffmann. In 1846 it was successfully performed in Paris, but Calderón's name was not mentioned. It was simply called "an adaptation from a Spanish author." In the 1920s, it was a great success in Hamburg, Frankfurt, and Berlin in a translation and adaptation by Otto Zoff.

In 1953 it experienced an unexpected revival at the Festival of Angers. Albert Camus made a prose translation of it, which more clearly reveals the timeless quality of this work and its author than all the earlier philologically accurate verse translations were able to do. It seems as if a new road toward the comprehension of Calderón has now been found. For despite all the praise that we may rightfully lavish on Calderón's linguistic excellence, the "strangeness," or alien nature, of his works may in large part be due to the essentially untranslatable form of his Spanish verse. Indeed, this difficulty is becoming more clear all the time.

Camus, in collaboration with Marcel Herrand, directed this production. Serge Reggiani and Maria Casarès played the principal roles. As for the stage sets and the style of the production in general, the fairy-tale quality of the baroque age was, following the spirit of our own age, intensified to colossal proportions. Let us not attempt to answer the question as to whether the "absurd severity" of the play really provided the stimulus that prompted Camus to undertake this work. Besides the gripping theatricality of the play, Camus may also have been attracted by the recognition that *The Devotion to the Cross* represented a credo that his own existentialist philosophy negated: the human being thrown into a world whose meaning is provided by suprahuman powers, who faces a destiny from which there is no escape. In antithesis to Camus's version of life, Calderón wrote out of the faith that the human being is not lost in the world's senselessness, that he is saved through grace. In this play grace is symbolized by the cross.

Life Is a Dream

In 1608 one of the most popular narratives of the Middle Ages, *Barlaam and Josephat*, appeared for the first time in Spanish. This work, which is supposed to be derived from a nonextant work, corresponds closely in its early part to the Buddha's life. It had appeared originally in the seventh century in Greek as a hymn of praise for the Christian way of life. In the course of the next five hundred years, variations of this narrative appeared in almost every language spoken by Christian peoples. An Islamic variation in Arabic was also known.

The narrative tells the story of Josephat, the son of an Indian king, who was raised in isolation from the world by his father because court astronomers had prophesied Josephat's conversion to Christianity. Despite his isolation, Josephat learns of the suffering of the world and has himself baptized by the Christian hermit Barlaam.

Both Lope de Vega and Calderón were stimulated to compose dramas on this subject. For Calderón, the story provided only the basic situation. *Life Is a Dream*, probably written in 1634, is considered Calderón's most profound drama. Since it is also one of his least timebound plays, it is one of his most frequently performed dramas. In this respect it is to be ranked with his *Phantom Lady* and *The Mayor Zalamea*. Critics have seen much in this work that Calderón himself did not intend. It is, however, precisely characteristic of Calderón's work as a whole that the philosophical dimensions of a play were seen only by later generations.

The plot is less complicated than that of his other plays. The location of action is Poland, which brings to mind the improbable geography of Shakespeare's Bohemia. There Rosaura—once again we have a girl disguised in male clothing—and her servant Clarín, the play's gracioso, find Prince Segismundo, dressed in fur pelts, chained and imprisoned in an isolated tower.

As was mentioned earlier, the human being dressed in fur pelts is a basic symbol in Calderón's work. The pelts suggest that the man wearing them has not found himself and is, therefore, still an animal, that he lives in the wilderness from which there is no escape.

The plot, which involves Rosaura, is unimportant to the basic idea of the drama. Calderón, who was first and foremost a dramatist, made use of this story because he wanted to present his world view dramatically. When Segismundo catches sight of Rosaura—she is the first woman whom he has ever seen—he is spellbound. His guardian Clotaldo has Rosaura and her companion imprisoned because no one is permitted to know the whereabouts of the prince.

Astolfo and Estrella, who are at the court of the king, want to join their claims to the throne through marriage. At this point the king, Basilio, tells them that he has a son, whom he has banished because the stars had prophesied that he would execute terrible acts of cruelty. Despite this warning, the king now decides that he will take the risk of testing his son—he will allow him to rule in his place for one day. Segismundo is drugged by a drink and brought to the palace. The prophecies of the stars seem to be confirmed: when Segismundo awakens from his drugged sleep, he murders a servant, attempts to rape Rosaura, and treats the king with contempt when the king chides him.

Once again drugged by a drink, Segismundo is returned to his tower. When he awakens, he does not know whether what he has experienced was dream or reality. What happened on that day seems to him more like illusion than reality. But there is one qualification to these feelings—Rosaura. Love is the single reality in a dream world. As a human response to divine grace, love in hand with grace forms a bridge over the abyss of the illusory and deceptive world, over the void. But this point of view is only intimated. More important is Clotaldo's simple conviction that man must always do the right thing even if this life is only a dream. This "doing the right thing," this moral imperative is the signpost that leads mankind out of chaos. Everything is uncertain. What is reality and what is illusion? What is the why and wherefore of our life? The will to goodness, however, gives this uncertainty a meaning and creates security. Segismundo's famous monologue concerning the nature of dream concludes the second act:

"In a word, this world of ours
Where men do dream what they do live,
Although they not see it so.
Thus I dream I be here now
Imprisoned here and tightly bound.
. . . .
So what is life? Nought but frenzy.
What is life but an illusion?
. . . .
Little is it fortune gives us.
For all of this is but a dream,
And the dreams themselves a dream."

The third act begins with the revolution. Soldiers
break into the tower in order to free Segismundo and
proclaim him king. A delightful idea, a variation of the
play's basic concept of the interchangeability of
everything earthly, is realized in the scene in which
the soldiers mistake Clarín for Segismundo and worship him as king.

Segismundo now thinks carefully about his course
of action. When he finally does resolve to become the
leader of the rebels in order to humiliate his father, he
decides to act "with deliberation and caution." Segismundo successfully surmounts the very first temptation during this second test. When Clotaldo refuses to
join the rebellion out of loyalty to the king, Segismundo controls his anger and lets him go his way. Self-
control is far more difficult for him when he meets
Rosaura again. It now seems impossible to him that a
dream could encompass so much beauty. But if
Rosaura is not a dream, then that day at court was no
dream. Doubt seems to overcome him once again. He

seeks help in platonic philosophy, but even the thought that Rosaura could be only a striking copy of an archetype (he says this literally)—even this seems hardly credible to him in view of her great beauty. But be that as it may, "Let love break all the laws of gallantry!" Let us make use of the time that is given to us; let us enjoy the moment!

Time as simulated reality. Out of his baroque-Catholic world view Calderón presented in a few lines a timeless truth that appears to us today to be exceptionally modern. All the more timebound is, conversely, the reason for Segismundo's change of heart. The truth that one should not sacrifice heaven's glory for pleasure on earth is not the decisive matter for Segismundo. Rather, he alters his decision because of the much more concrete realization that Rosaura's honor must remain unsullied. She must not be sacrificed to a dream.

A humorous interlude follows the tragical love scene. During the battle between father and son Clarín holes up in a cave to await the outcome. He is concerned only with the preservation of his life. But a stray bullet hits him:

> "Since there is no hiding place
> To protect you from fate's fell stroke—
> That would save you from the stars' fury.
> Seek as you might fleeing to rescue,
> Seek it in most dread despair,
> It is to death you are delivered
> If God so wills it, you're doomed to fall."

But Clarín's end, which can be interpreted in terms of the basic idea of the play as the end of a human being who lacks a will, is not the important element in this scene. What is more important is the way in which Calderón undertook Clarín's characterization. Here Clarín as the gracioso is a representative of the ordinary, practical man. His peasant cunning is no guarantee of a happy end, as is usually true in the comedia. In a world in which honor and virtue are recognized to be more real than wealth and power, in a world of excess (a frequent epithet used to describe seventeenth-century Spain) the calculating person must suffer shipwreck.

After resisting the temptations posed by Clotaldo and Rosaura, Segismundo must now face the decisive confrontation with his father. When the vanquished king attempts to kneel before his son, the son raises him up and himself kneels before his father. He has accepted grace; he has decided to do what is right. As a Christian, to do right means to forgive as well as to recognize the prevailing order. He also conquers his emotions and gives Rosaura in marriage to Astolfo, a man who had insulted her honor. This action is dictated by the code of honor of the age, which, let us again stress here, was primarily religious, not social. Segismundo himself asks for Estrella's hand.

These marriages, which seem absurd to us, were necessary to Calderón in two ways. First, such marriages at the finale were required by Calderón's public just as such marriages are required at operetta finales. Second, they represented the restoration of order, since Rosaura's honor is vindicated and Segismundo is married to a princess who is his social equal. The condemnation of the officer who first proclaimed Segismundo king seems especially severe to us. But this also signifies a restoration of order. No matter what the appearance, every rebellion meant for Calderón a rebellion against order, and therefore, a rebellion in a wider sense against the divine cosmos. If we bear in mind that Calderón's dramatic technique was largely one of illustration, so that persons and actions were of an archetypical kind, then the contrived effect of the play's concluding scene can be seen in a quite different light. Even our sympathy for the condemned soldier disappears if we view this character as an example rather than an individual human being.

Because the monologues, which are often pages long, are often abridged in contemporary productions, the rigorous construction of the play does not always come across. The two tests occur within Segismundo's extensive monologues. Moreover, these monologues can be considered to be quasi-independent poems, since Calderón employed a different meter in these verses from that used elsewhere in the play. In each case, they sum up Segismundo's experience: the first monologue contains lament; the second, doubt; the third, perception of truth. The two tests, that is to say, the action of the second and third acts, are parallel in form and in content. Segismundo fails the first test —he wants to murder his tutor, rape the woman he loves, and cast his father from the throne.

In the second test, however, after experiencing insight into the dreamlike nature of existence and after heeding Clotaldo's counsel about the virtue of doing the right thing, Segismundo encounters the same people in the same order. This time he allows Clotaldo, who would rather die by Segismundo's hand than join the rebellion, to return to the enemy camp. Now that it would be easy for Segismundo to win Rosaura's love, as their conversation indicates, he conquers his own inclinations for the sake of her honor. The king, who has humbled himself before his son, is raised up while Segismundo himself kneels. In other words, the first test is complemented by the second. Segismundo as well as the other characters reverses his actions.

The rigorousness of this drama's construction corresponds to its internal content. The "struggle for existence" gives way to the "struggle for the preservation of existing order." The "will to power" is supplanted by the "will to powerlessness," which paradoxically makes manifest man's real power over his own passions. This basic line never obtrudes through the play as naked construction. Calderón has disguised his scaffolding with the most manifold kinds of ornament and image so that it takes a precise analysis to reveal the simple beauty of the form of the play.

The meaning of life lies in "doing right." But the meaning of life is not synonymous with the reality of life. If *Life Is a Dream* deals with absolute reality at all, this reality is transcendent reality, not earthly reality. Human life, indeed, everything that man perceives through his senses, remains just as mysterious for the writer of *Life Is a Dream* as it does for men of our own age. Calderón's absolutes lie in the realm of faith, not in philosophy.

The fundamental idea of this play, doubt in the nature of reality, is not of Christian origin. This skepticism comes from the Orient, in which it is a common assumption in religious thought. Calderón, or perhaps one of his predecessors, translated this eastern concept into valid Christian terms. It was the Indian origin not only of the plot of this drama but also of its fundamental idea that aroused Schopenhauer's strong interest in this work. It is also of interest that the motif of a man who awakens in a strange environment is of eastern origin. Shakespeare employed this theme in a cheerful context in his play *The Taming of the Shrew*. It is by no means unusual to find motifs of oriental derivation in Spanish literature.

Life Is a Dream has been given various interpretations by modern directors. For some directors, Calderón's theatrical ambience is of primary significance. Others focus on the logical consistency of his work as well as the relevance of his work to our own age. If one leaves aside the baroque elements of his drama, one recognizes that in Calderón's work the drama of human life is being played out. According to natural law and to astrology, man is destined to become man's enemy. His goal is power. Only after recognizing his impotence is man really ready to think. To think in this sense is to reflect upon the meaning of life and to speculate on the nature of reality. If reality does not exist, then to give oneself to reality is synonymous with plunging into an abyss. What is left to man is to ferret out a moral law within himself. For Calderón, a believing Catholic, this was imperative. For modern man, finding this moral law is only an option. Even the recognition of goodness is still not Calderón's final word; what is of the essence is that the human being, acting out of his own free will, decides in favor of virtue. The individual's willing acceptance of God's grace signifies his participation in the absolute.

That Segismundo acquires insight and knowledge through dream once again reveals this play's amazing anticipation of spheres of experience that we associate with our times. Although psychoanalysis is too often applied inappropriately, one of the most important dream plays in world literature requires at least a brief reference to it. The significance of the images of the cave and the dark tower, and, even more, the phenomenon of truth being perceived in dream, are elements in contemporary psychoanalytic thought. Psychoanalysts tell us that much that goes on in our unconscious minds is more real in our sense of the word than the reality experienced by our conscious minds.

Calderón turned this play into an *auto sacramental* (as he did some of his other plays), around 1677. At first sight, this *auto* would appear to be a commentary on the philosophy expressed in the first version. The characters become types or allegories. But on closer inspection we see that although the action is the same in the two versions, the theme is different. Basilio, the king, is now God. This in itself changes the intellectual presuppositions. God cannot become guilty as a king can. He cannot, like a king, attempt to circumvent the law of the stars by exiling his son. The significance of the two tests being authored by two beings— the first by the king, that is, a human being, the second by God—is thereby abrogated.

Wisdom tries to prevent man from bringing evil into the world by attempting to hold him fast in a state of unconsciousness (in the cave that is synonymous with the earth itself). But love does not allow this condition to last. If free will has been given to the human being, his life cannot be directed so long as he has not yet realized himself.

In this *auto* man does recognize the dreamlike nature of all existence, but his hope lies in awakening into a better life. The personified Dream itself provides him with the answer: "But that will mean death." Incapable of vanquishing death, since he has earned it by becoming guilty, the human being needs the help of Wisdom, which now allows itself to be captured and crucified for his sake.

Life Is a Dream is one of the most frequently and most internationally performed of all of Calderón's works. It was premiered in 1635 at the court theater of Madrid. As early as 1651 it was performed in Amsterdam. In 1654 the first German performance took place in Hamburg. In 1674, it was given in Dresden under the title *Prince Sigismundo*. Master Velten's troupe produced it in 1690 as *Prince Sigismund in Poland*. In 1717, it was first performed in French and Italian. In 1741, the play was performed in Jesuit houses as a didactic work. After it was presented in Weimar on 3 March 1812, in a production directed by Goethe, the play became an established item of the German theater.

In 1881, to commemorate the two-hundredth anniversary of Calderón's death, *Life Is a Dream* was performed in the two leading theaters of the Spanish capital, the Teatro Real and the Teatro Español. One wonders how these two productions managed to depict through Segismundo the "laming of our conscience by the chains of absolutism," which is the way the dramas were described in the festival edition of the journal *Dia*.

The Vienna Burgtheater undertook a production of *Life Is a Dream*, which became famous at the end of the nineteenth century.

Rossini employed Calderón's material for his opera *Sigismondo*. A German opera using Calderón's plot had already been produced in 1693.

A varied critical reception was accorded to the 1950

production of this play in Munich; the production was mounted to celebrate the three-hundred-and-fiftieth birthday of Calderón. The director Peter Lühr seems to have followed the interpretation of the translator Eugen Gürstner, which is that *Life Is a Dream* "can be played as if it were an opera without music." The play is "life itself, whose dreamlike nature Calderón has movingly revealed." The stage sets also implemented this musical-baroque conception. Projecting an effect of dreamlike unreality, they were able to give the illusion of "disappearing into air" when raised aloft. A different kind of symbolism was employed in the last scene, in which the actors performed on a gigantic, broken statue of Mars.

Walter Kiaulehn's observations about the composition of the audience at this Munich production are interesting. First, he noted that one saw old and young people in the theater, but not the middle-aged, a fact that might lead one to conclude that the middle-aged could not muster up any interest in Calderón. Second, he made a comment that hints at something more significant under its apparent frivolousness: "The advantage of being a Catholic Christian is never made to seem as fortunate and as compellingly clear as it does to the Catholic Christian who sits in Calderón's theater. The Protestants think all evening long of Shakespeare." One could enlarge upon this statement by substituting for Catholic Christian a theatergoer who is naive, in the best sense of the word; for Protestant one could substitute that theatergoer who has remained inside the conventions of the classical-psychological theater.

Ulrich Erfurth succeeded in projecting the philosophical-spiritual element of *Life Is a Dream* in his

Düsseldorf production of the 1951–52 season. The revolt was subordinated, but not to favor a noncommital dream-romanticism. Instead the interpretation focused on the intellectual content of the play. That this production did not seem to be abstract and contrived was assured by Calderón's poetic power. The actor who portrayed Segismundo, Horst Caspar, made the major single contribution to the play's effectiveness. He carried out totally Calderón's conception of the "yet unborn human being dressed in fur pelts"—man in his cave who first of all must realize himself. He did not play the role of a historical Polish prince who has been held captive by his father. He played the human being per se, "the desperate questioner who, filled with wonder at his own existence, did not so much enjoy power as test it out, a man who was from the very beginning on the road to realizing himself."

Segismundo, as Caspar played him, was a man who just awakening tried out his own power with the curiosity of a boy, a man who at the very beginning had not even been conscious of the burden of his chains. This test meant suffering and he had to accept sufferings. So far as we know, no other actor has ever expressed so clearly and with such "intensification of emotions, from gentleness to explosiveness," the passive nature of this Calderón hero. To be chosen, both with respect to temptation and to self-conquest, became, in Caspar's interpretation, the tragedy of the isolated human being. Out of his isolation he found the way to do the right thing, the only way he could escape from the thicket of a humanity that never understood him.

Heinrich Koch's Hamburg production of the following year found it hard to hold its own against the success of the Düsseldorf production. Will Quadflieg as Segismundo did not portray the suffering human being in his isolation. Rather he projected a man hungering for life. He represented the animal nature of man that must first be restrained by dreamlike experience. His Segismundo became a rebel not out of logical reflection but out of an instinctual thirst for revenge. Since, in the play, the instinctual urgency of Segismundo's actions is emphasized, and this urgency is an inherent part of Segismundo's character, his conduct was not individualized, rather decreed by fate. Thus, Quadflieg's interpretation also was true to the intellectual conception of Calderón's work.

The 1964–65 Düsseldorf production by the painter Jean-Pierre Ponnelle, who also designed his own sets, has become one of the most intellectually lucid versions of this play. A star-studded cupola provided the basic motif that dominated the stage in every scene, whether the action took place in the wilderness or in the king's chambers. This cupola symbolized the fundamental idea of this production: the power of the stars. Even beyond this, it symbolized the power of the cosmos to determine man's fate. Without demonstrating any forced craving for originality, Ponnelle succeeded in offering a production whose nature was almost choreographic, one characterized by a carefully planned harmony of dialogue, gesture, and movement.

In the United States, too, *Life Is a Dream* has been the most frequently performed of Calderón's plays. In 1953 it was performed, along with *The Mayor of Zalamea*, at the Broadhurst Theater in New York. Both productions, presented by Alejandro Ulloa and his troupe, were given in Spanish.

In March 1964 the Teatro Español of New York

presented a "bilingual" production of *Life Is a Dream* at the Astor Place Playhouse. The Spanish version, directed by José Crespo, and the English version, in a translation by Roy Campbell, directed by Jay Broad, were presented on alternating evenings. The sets, costumes, and style of the two productions were in marked contrast: José Crespo directed the original drama in a traditional, conventional Spanish style; in the English-language version, the actors performed on an open raised platform much like that used by the Elizabethan traveling troupes. Herbert Kupferberg of the *New York Herald Tribune*, in his review of 20 March 1964, noted a significant difference in the two approaches: he described the Spanish production as a "seventeenth-century costume drama illuminated by the poetry and color of its native tongue," while the English version, unable to rely on the lyrical quality of Calderón's verse, "sought to extract every ounce of action and even of comedy suggested by Calderón's lines."

After the opening of Crespo's production, Walter Kerr wrote in the *New York Herald Tribune*, on 18 March 1964, that in spite of the barrier presented by the use of Spanish to the English-speaking theatergoer, much was still communicated by the superior acting:

> I could listen to Raul Davila [Segismundo], as a forlorn heir to the throne locked away in a mountain fastness, give vent to his anger in a most fascinating way. I understood that his anger rose from the intolerable isolation in which he found himself and in which he had lived his whole youth through. But it seemed—with the winged, uncommunicative words flying by so fiercely—to be due

to, and to be aimed at, so much more than that. It seemed an anger directed at emotion itself, at all of the things this imprisoned prince was feeling—as though he had been through quite enough turmoil to no useful purpose, as though he had come to hate his own futile sensibilities.

More recently, *Life Is a Dream* was staged by John Emigh, with music by Gerald Shapiro, at the Faunce House Theatre at Brown University in Providence, Rhode Island. For this production, the translation by Edwin Honig was used. In March 1972 the Yale Repertory Theater offered a new production, using Roy Campbell's translation. Jacques Burdick directed. Writing in the *New York Times* on 21 March 1972, Mel Gussow wrote about this production:

> *Life Is a Dream* is a masterpiece deserving revival and re-study, and the Yale Repertory rises to the challenge. Among its timeless themes are the confusion between reality and illusion, the competition between parent and child, the confrontation of the original with the copy, the eclipse of the individual by history. . . . Read Segismund as you will—as the sleeping prince, or stand-in for a larger issue. Today, he could in fact be the black man, subjugated by whites, released suddenly and willfully—with repression always at arm's reach. . . . Burdick transmits Calderón undistorted and with considerable distinction.

Love, The Greatest Enchantment

Love, The Greatest Enchantment is said to have been written in the same year that Calderón became director of the outdoor theater at Buen Ritiro, 1635. It is today considered to be the most perfect baroque work of that period; for it is a veritable feast of music, technical effects, visual delights, and, above all, poetry. A play about enchantment, this splendid production must have seemed to the theatergoer a work created by magic.

Classical antiquity meant for Calderón material on which he could give reign to his imagination. His was a visual rather than an intellectual interest in antiquity. If one can at all speak of antiquity as having produced mythological works similar to this drama, they can be seen primarily in Apuleius's fairy-tale characters or Ovid's *Metamorphoses*. Calderón was only acquainted with classical antiquity in the watered-down version of Italian writers. Calderón stands closest to Ariosto, although Ariosto naturally had a different relationship to the ancient cultural past of his own people. That

Spain's own Roman past had not been entirely forgotten, can be seen in the fact that Calderón speaks of the Spanish Seneca in his works. To Calderón, ancient Greece was just as remote and nebulous as the Orient or any kind of vague and indeterminate fairy-tale land. As in many of his so-called historical dramas, the figures of the mythological plays move according to a Spanish ceremonial pattern. The rule of the game for all of Calderón's heroes, whether gallant love affairs or ultimate ethical decisions were involved, was specifically Spanish and baroque.

Few reworkings of classical material that have been undertaken in other ages, particularly in our own day, possess the degree of modernity that Calderón gave to this material. In his day, people did not consider that such modernization was irreverent. Neither did they impute it to his lack of classical knowledge. Baroque pastoral idylls, romantic journeys (known and loved elements in numerous popular narratives of the day), in combination with the medieval conception of love, provided effective elements of *Love, The Greatest Enchantment*. Its external plot was adapted from an episode in the Odyssey.

The style of the play as a whole was dominated by the theatrical machinery of the court theater at Buen Retiro, which is said to have terrified Calderón when he first saw it but which—brilliant man of the theater that he was—he very soon learned how to subordinate to his own purposes. For he only set this machinery into action, or rather allowed it to produce its most striking effects, when decisive dramatic turning points were involved. Even these new technical developments were subordinated to the primary purpose of Calderón's art, the visual representation of spiritual and intellectual matters. The result was a theater for the eyes that outdid anything before it but yet did not permit its external effects to overshadow the inner content of a drama.

It would, to be sure, be an overestimation of the intellectual content of this play to analyze it as a masked form of a philosophical idea. We know that Calderón was here primarily concerned with festivity. It is also obvious, however, that he did not design even this type of festival play without giving consideration to its spiritual content. In accordance with his own world view, even the plot of this play ultimately expressed the indestructibility of the great cosmic order. Moreover, Ulysses had long been a stock type in Spanish literature, the man who had conquered his sensuality.

Utilizing the kind of landscape provided by the park of Buen Retiro with its many ponds, the action of this play begins with a storm at sea. Only through their prayers to Juno is it possible for Ulysses and his comrades to save themselves. But the coast on which they land brings new dangers. A pack of wild animals —popular figures in the baroque theater—meets them. These animals turn out to be harmless. The lion himself indicates to Ulysses, by means of very human gestures, that it would be best for him to sail on. But it is already too late. Ulysses's comrades, who had roamed inland, return; they have been transformed into animals.

The sorceress Circe then appears with a large retinue. She wants to bewitch Ulysses by means of a magic potion. But Juno has taken the precaution of sending a bouquet of flowers to Ulysses through Iris, who in a most theatrical fashion appears on a rainbow.

The bouquet functions as an antidote to Circe's potion. Ulysses touches the drink with this bouquet, a
flame hisses upward, and Ulysses is safe from Circe's
power. But as a man bred with Spanish courtesy,
Ulysses accepts her invitation to visit her magical palace. He asks only for the return of his comrades to
their human form, and for the liberation of a pair of
lovers whom Circe had transformed into two trees.

As the audience anticipates, Ulysses and Circe find
themselves overcome by love. But until this love is
actually confessed, we become witness to the most
delightful social games; indeed, life itself seems to become a game that is played according to set rules.
Neither wishes to confess his love to the other. They
begin to question each other in the form of riddles.
Ulysses's final act of dissimulating his feelings takes
place when he suggests that they play a game in which
he will pretend that he is in love with Circe. As often
occurs in Calderón's more serious dramas, a fantastic
confusion arises in which no one knows any longer
what is merely a game and what is the truth. A simulated enemy attack tests both Ulysses and his rival
Arsidas, who is also in love with Circe. Ulysses goes
out to meet the enemies while Arsidas remains near to
Circe to protect her. Since no one can decide whose
action has demonstrated more love, the inevitable duel
ensues. Circe separates the combatants on the grounds
that a spiritual conflict cannot be decided with weap-
ons.

In the third act, Ulysses and Circe celebrate their
love after Ulysses has confessed his love in coded form
by means of a tale concerning a hunt for herons. This
tale is, incidentally, one of Calderón's most beautiful
poems. Fearing that Ulysses will now want to remain

on the island in a state of inactive pleasure, his comrades secretly place Achilles's armor, which had been presented to him at Troy where he was deemed the worthiest of the Greeks, near their sleeping leader. When Ulysses awakens, the spirit of Achilles himself appears and recalls him to responsibility. He pulls himself together and departs with his comrades. Circe tries to bring him back by causing a magical storm, but Galathea's appearance signifies the fact that Ulysses is now sailing under divine protection. For the desperate Circe, nothing remains but to destroy herself. In a magnificent finale, Circe sinks both herself and her whole island dominion into the sea. The volcano Aetna then arises out of the waves, spewing flames. A ballet concludes the play.

That the graciosos have not been forgotten in such a fantastic festival play is a foregone conclusion. Indeed, they have an essential role to play. Named Clarín and Leporello, they are Ulysses's comrades. The scene between Clarín and Brutamonte, a giant from Circe's realm, is most delightful. But even more amusing is Clarín's transformation into a monkey. Leporello captures him and is full of pride that he will now be able to show off an exotic animal when he returns to Ithaca. The theatrical effectiveness of this scene derives above all from the fact that the public understands the words of Clarín, who has been transformed into a monkey, whereas it is made clear to the audience that his own comrade Leporello does not. Leporello immediately begins to train his monkey. The role of man turned into monkey must have been a particularly attractive task for a clown. Only when he accidentally looks into a mirror is Clarín freed from enchantment and transformed back into his human form.

It is well known that those scenes from *Love, The Greatest Enchantment* that were played with crudeness and vulgarity enjoyed the greatest measure of public success in the first productions outside of Spain of this play. But this inartistic manner of popularizing Calderón is not to be seen as only unfortunate. It played an important role in increasing Calderón's influence on foreign theater outside of Spain. If this was less true of the art theater in Europe, whose founders attempted to interpret and to give proper value to Calderón's art but failed to elicit a strongly favorable response in their audiences, it certainly held true for the much wider area of popular theater. His influence ranged from the school theaters of the various religious orders to the heyday of the Viennese folk theater. The nineteenth-century Austrian playwright Ferdinand Raimund, without knowing it, had more success in creating works in the true spirit of Calderón than did Franz Grillparzer, who attempted a direct literary adaptation of Calderón's works. Raimund's magical fairy tales, with their alternations of pathos and comedy, are, as it were, the last bourgeois incarnation of Calderón's aristocratic and baroque theater. The scene between Clarín and Brutamonte in *Love, The Greatest Enchantment* could well be a scene in Raimund's works.

Calderón later created an *auto sacramental* out of this work, in which the hero, Ulysses, once again represents man in general. His comrades are his Senses, which are all transformed into animals by Circe, who symbolizes sin. The bouquet that Juno had given to Ulysses in order to save him becomes the bouquet of virtue. The dew upon the flowers stands for the life blood of the lamb. The meal that Ulysses eats at the end of the *auto*, as opposed to the feast that he consumes with Circe in the earlier drama, is the sacrament. Thus this *auto* by means of its skillful allegorization also ends with men's salvation through the sacrament.

On Midsummer Night of the year 1635, this most magnificent of all of Calderón's festival plays was premiered in the park of Buen Retiro. The Italian theater architect Cosme Lotti assumed the technical direction of this production. The stage was set on a small island in an artificial pond; the island was probably surrounded by flat boats on which other settings were constructed. A storm at sea was reproduced by means of paddle wheels; Ulysses' ship really appeared to be tossed on the waves. All of the play's transformations took place before the spectator's eyes. The climax of this art of stage settings was to be seen in Circe's water procession, made up of swimming nixes and exotic fish who sprinkled the spectators with perfumed water from fountains. As a concluding effect, the entire island sank into the water; in its place arose a fire-spitting mountain.

The accomplishment of these theatrical wonders seems to us today to be inconceivable considering the modest technology available to the theater in the seventeenth century. But authentic sources tell us that the art of illusion practiced by Italian architects was so great that it could reduce the most sophisticated public to a state of childlike astonishment. The cost of such performances was correspondingly enormous. This production was repeated three times, which was proof of its success. According to one source, each act of the play was allegedly performed by a different favorite troupe of Philip IV and in a different area of the park. Four years later the play was performed in Madrid.

In recent times, this play had its first performance at the Deutsches Schauspielhaus in Hamburg in 1955 under the direction of Heinrich Koch. Contrary to expectation, Koch presented this play as "conventional baroque theater." He probably took particular care not to project intellectual traits into this festival play, which was virtually intoxicated with love.

The Darmstadt production of the play under the direction of Gustav Rudolf Sellner during the 1956–57 season was held in far higher regard. It is indeed possible that this play gained admission to the German repertory through this staging. Aside from the controversial modern interpretation of the play's conclusion, Sellner succeeded in revealing Calderón's fundamental intellectual conception. Moreover, he accomplished this without having to renounce in the least the element of magic theater, that aspect of this work that gives it its greatest charm.

Sellner used August Wilhelm Schlegel's translation, which "thickened Calderón's baroque imagination with romantic fusion." But this "romantic fusion" did not obtrude. What came through was the presence of a genuine baroque imagination that, to be sure, was adapted to the sensibility of our own age. Sellner approached the work from a visual point of view—the music and the actors' dancing movements were harmoniously integrated with the text. What he produced was baroque antiquity, delicately parodied by the play's Spanish costumes. The stage sets were abstract, but it was precisely "out of this discrepancy between the three worlds (classical antiquity, baroque, and modern) that a new, timeless world arose—the world of fantasy, a world of more profound significance" (Wilhelm Ringelband).

Sellner saw the basic idea as the expression of the tragic division between the masculine and the feminine principles. Despite the flight of the man and the suicide of the woman for the sake of love, the play presents in a boldly paradoxical manner an apotheosis of precisely this love. Sellner has been much criticized for having made a "contemporary" change in the ending of the play. That Ulysses finally follows Achilles's military command and rejects Circe is immoral from the viewpoint of our own time. In Sellner's production this action, an expression of the masculine principle, which betrays love for honor's sake, is condemned. He has Circe say: "It has been given into our hands, into the hands of women, to bring love into the world and with it order." In so doing, Sellner took the sting out of Calderón's poetic paradox. The ideal of love, tragic because it cannot be fulfilled in reality, is here exchanged for an inartistic, didactic final assertion.

Moreover, the reasons for Circe's furious demand that the gods now destroy the unfaithful Ulysses remain unexplained in Calderón's text. The explanation, according to the present version, that Circe's sacrifice—in transforming herself from a sorceress into a loving woman—is for nought does not hold up. This explanation is invalid both artistically and intellectually because Calderón was writing out of the tragic recognition that the male and the female principles cannot be unified. What was to have been a well-meant retouching of a militaristic body of ideas by shifting the weights disrupts the meaning. In Sellner's production the end of what is a festive and cheerful play becomes essentially tragic. For, as Calderón ends the play, love is not superior to all enchantment. Through Galathea's final words, he allows Ulysses to be celebrated as the victor over a seductive adventuress. Calderón's conclusion led directly to a final ballet and therefore to a jubilant conclusion of the play, for he did not want to end it with despair.

The Constant Prince

      This play, like *Love, The Greatest Enchantment*, was probably also written in the year 1635. Its subject matter had already been used by Lope de Vega. The German romantic poets gave no higher praise to any other of Calderón's dramas. And of all the works that are still performed today, *The Constant Prince* seems to be the play most indebted to the spirit of the age in which it was written. Goethe, who read this work aloud in the house of Johanna Schopenhauer, is said to have suddenly interrupted his reading because he was overcome with emotion. "If poetry were to be lost from the world," he said, "one could resurrect it once again through this play alone." And Joseph von Eichendorff called it "one of the most glorious tragedies ever written." Perhaps it appealed to the taste of the German romantics just by the fact that it presented a historical subject in a timeless poetic way rather than by baroque-izing it.

      Fernando, the "constant prince," the brother of the

Portuguese King Duarte, was one of the heroes of the Reconquista, the centuries-long struggle between the Christians and the Moors on the Iberian peninsula. He was taken prisoner during the siege of Tangiers in 1438 and died five years later in slavery. As early as 1470 he was canonized.

Since this play is a drama of martyrdom, it does not begin with the customary duel or any similar kind of activity. It begins with the chorus of the Christian slaves. Fénix, the Moorish princess of Fez, loves Muley, commander-in-chief of the king of Fez. For political reasons, however, her father had destined her to be the wife of Tarudante, the king of Morocco. In the battle of Tangiers, Muley is taken prisoner by the Portuguese Prince Fernando. He confesses his amorous sorrows to the prince, who thereupon in knightly fashion returns him as a free man to his lady.

The vicissitudes of war change, and Fernando is taken prisoner. At first, the king of Fez treats him with honor, since he hopes to bargain for the return of Ceuta, a city that has been occupied by the Christians, as ransom for Fernando. Fernando tears up the authorization of King Duarte, who is willing to accept the terms of the king of Fez. He cannot take it upon his conscience to allow the Christians to lose a city merely for his own personal sake. The king of Fez treats him henceforth with brutality. Muley, who wishes to free Fernando out of gratitude, is now placed in a situation in which he must suffer great anguish of conscience, for he has been ordered personally by the king to keep watch over Fernando.

The war breaks out anew. In a moving scene in which the king of Fez wishes to demonstrate his power to his future son-in-law, the ruler of Morocco,

Fernando is seen begging for bread. When the king of Fez calls him into the royal presence, he collapses and dies. But the spirit of this martyred prince, clothed in the red cloak of his order, now rides at the head of the Portuguese army and leads his people to victory. The king of Fez is now compelled to hand over the body of Fernando as ransom for his daughter and her fiancé, both of whom have been captured. The king of Fez, however, has also been gripped by the miracle of the vision. Thus he does not reject the king of Portugal's request that Fénix be married to Muley. At the end, the king of Fez orders everyone to accompany the coffin of Prince Fernando in order thereby to show him final honor.

So much for the external plot, which, according to historical fact, may seem to be a romanticizing of Prince Fernando. But the martyr who gave his life almost cheerfully for his Christian faith, was, for Calderón, historical reality, not an idealization. This cheerful renunciation, however, arouses sympathy for the hero even in modern audiences. For Fernando is not one of those renunciants, as they appear in the classical dramas of France and Germany, who always arouse the suspicion of being theatrically contrived. Ultimately, his cheerfulness provides further proof of the passivity of Calderón's heroes. They themselves do not struggle for greatness; rather, they are given the chance to bear fate with dignity. Man himself does not construct his fate, as in the drama of character; rather, he receives fate as a gift, even though this fate may bring him sorrow. His greatness lies in the fact that he nevertheless receives his fate with gratitude. His free will has made proper use of grace. Because of this, the dead prince is still able to bring victory to his people.

On the basis of this view of life, Karl Vossler has termed Calderón a poet of freedom, "though to be sure, of a freedom seen as action, as self-liberation through greatness of character and not of a freedom which one possesses, enjoys, and administers like a liberal bourgeois."

Only if we approach this work with sympathetic understanding for its historical context, shall we be able to recognize its total beauty. So long as we view history solely from the vantage point of our day, much of what is in the play will remain hidden and much that we see will appear absurd. It should be noted here that sympathetic understanding of history stands diametrically opposed to romanticizing history. Nor is Calderón's play romantic in the sense in which German post-romantics defined the word romantic. In Calderón's day, the battles of the Reconquista still lived so immediately in the memory of the people that this play is to be seen as one of Calderón's very few historical dramas rather than as a romantic recreation. Nor does this contradict the simultaneous representation of the miraculous, that is, the vision of the dead prince leading his army to victory. For Calderón, the miraculous played an essential part in history.

The basic ethical foundations of Calderón's image of the world, that is, honor and religion, are in no other of his works so inseparably interwoven. Honor is a knightly virtue. The Moor sets as much value on this virtue as the Christian does. Indeed, concern with this virtue pervades medieval literature. But to find this universal concept of honor in Calderón's works is of interest to us in a double sense. First, since in Calderón's day Islamic culture was still woven into the texture of Spain, Calderón must have been well acquainted with the Islamic way of life, which he was able to convey in his work with authenticity. Secondly, in regarding the virtues of Spain's enemies as highly as he did those of his own compatriots, Calderón demonstrated his political objectivity. This objectivity seems to be almost incomprehensible in view of the totalitarian position of the Spanish church, its persecution of the Jews and the Moors as well as the prevailing contempt for all people of mixed blood.

From what has been said above, it is clear that this drama of honor belongs as much to the Moor Muley as to the Christian Ferando. The scenes that show how Muley wishes to save Fernando but is prevented from doing so because his duty to his king is more important than his duty to a friend—these scenes provide the dramatic representation of a code of honor that is international.

The drama of faith and the possibility of martyrdom are, however, reserved only for the Christian hero in Calderón's works.

Eichendorff once broke out in an exultant cry of praise for Calderón's presentation of the vision of the prince after his death, writing: "It is the triumph of the eternal over the temporal, presented with such tragic power as has never been achieved in any play by a writer of any other nation." To a certain extent this statement expresses that particular enthusiasm for religion that was part of German romanticism. But such a statement made by a poet of Eichendorff's stature also reveals a true recognition of the unusual poetic beauty of this work, a work that would otherwise have hardly been able to withstand the passage of time so successfully.

There is no information, not even the year, about the premiere of *The Constant Prince*. The first recorded performance of this work is Goethe's famous production, using a translation by Schlegel, in Weimar in 1811. After the performance, Goethe himself issued the following enthusiastic judgment: "This time we have presented a play that was written more than two hundred years ago in a completely different part of the world and for a public with a totally different educational background—and this with the freshness of something just out of the oven."

The initiator of the Düsseldorf premiere on 9 April 1833, Karl Immermann, was even more enthusiastic about his production than Goethe was about his: "What a play! One does not tire of watching and admiring it! In this single work the great Catholic poet has hoisted himself into a sphere that has not even been reached by Shakespeare. No production of any work either before or since Calderón's day has even been remotely able to approach this tragedy." That this play still frequently appears in the repertory of contemporary theater may well give proof of its timeless poetic value.

In 1957, in Protestant Hamburg, the timelessness of this work was demonstrated. Here the play's Catholicism was not viewed as a topical type of denominationalism. It was approached in a more objective manner. Even if the critics were sparing in their praise and offered many objections to the production, the play nevertheless enjoyed a very great public success—it was referred to as an altogether "great evening in the theater." In his review of the Hamburg production Werner Knöth went to the heart of the matter. He wrote that this play is primarily concerned with "the freedom of a Christian human being." Fernando in prison signifies man in his hopelessness. He liberates himself from this situation by accepting his hopelessness, by suffering consciously, and by accepting this suffering as having meaning. Knöth wrote: "Don Fernando has become the very model of that doctrine of Christian existentialism that once again has taken on so much meaning for us today."

In 1966, Jerzy Grotowski produced an adaptation of *The Constant Prince* in his Breslau Theater Laboratory. This version was also presented at the annual international theater festival in Paris. In 1969 Grotowski and his Theater Laboratory—or, as he calls it, his "theater of poverty"—were brought to the United States under the auspices of the Brooklyn Academy of Music. For their American debut the company offered *The Constant Prince* (in Polish) at the Washington Square Methodist Church in Greenwich Village. Grotowski, who is in the tradition of Antonin Artaud and his theater of cruelty, found in this play an example for his thesis that the theater can lead us to self-knowledge only by "visualizing existential borderline situations." Only after man has totally surrendered himself does he find himself.

With his choice of this play, Grotowski offered renewed proof of the closeness of Calderón's drama to the spirit of our age, for few of the great European dramas of the past would have lent themselves to Grotowski's treatment. The condition of being delivered up and the individual's overcoming of this situation by his acceptance is elucidated in Grotowski's theater, although new techniques are utilized. The language here is of secondary importance. The mimic aspect, even so far as sound is concerned, is dominant. Fernando is thrust into confrontation with the roaring, sadistic masses. The cries of these crowds are sometimes intensified into litanies. The play becomes a ritual; martyrdom becomes symbolic of the birth of a new kind of man, a man who comes to the truth of his feelings only after having been made to suffer in the extreme. As Edith Oliver wrote in the *New Yorker* (25 October 1969):

> Near the end the Prince sinks to his knees. His face . . . becomes a mask. "The Prince's ecstasy is his suffering." These six words from the synopsis are expressed by one indelible look by Ryszard Cieslak [the Prince], as his eyes become unfocused, almost blind with inward gaze. His emotion has become as disembodied as that of his torturers.

Baroque wisdom and modern insights have been theatrically unified in this production. Once again the intentions of the modern director accord with those of the earlier dramatist. Both are solely concerned with existential questions. All concrete accusations, even those of social concern, seem to both of these men insignificant, or at least beyond the scope of the theater's tasks.

The most unusual demands were made on the actors. Total control of the body was necessary, since the "theory of intensification had to be converted into physical reality through the physical body." No more than one hundred people were admitted to each performance of the Polish production. A stage was constructed to resemble a rectangular bullring, and was surrounded by a high wooden wall. The audience, seated on wooden benches above this wall, looked down on the play. The program notes for the American audience commented on this structure: "The arrangement of stage and audience is a sort of intermediary between a circus arena and operating room. . . . What one sees below can be regarded either as a cruel game in a Roman circus or as a surgical operation in the manner of Rembrandt's *The Anatomy Lesson of Dr. Tulp*."

Clive Barnes, in his review in the *New York Times* (18 October 1969), wrote:

> Grotowski realizes . . . a new relationship between the actor and the audience. . . . It is a theater where the playwright undertakes a new function —the classically critical function of interpreter. . . . We are the audience at a bullfight. We are glancing down, in all the quality of our momentary godhead, at an event that does not concern us. A man's predestined death. But we also know that we cannot change the drama's pattern, so that our godlike sense of observation subsides chaotically into a realistic view of our innocent impotence.

The Daughter of Air

Calderón is said to have completed the first part of *The Daughter of Air* in 1650, the second part fourteen years later. The design of the first part clearly pointed to the second. To speak here of a historical chronicle, as is often done, in my opinion leads away from the meaning of the play. Between about 810 and 806 B.C., Queen Sammu-ramat energetically ruled Assyria in place of her son Adadnirari III. Her image was preserved for posterity chiefly through Greek legends of a Queen Semiramis. The story of this extraordinary woman was also told throughout the Middle Ages in many variations. Calderón saw the heroine of his play as the legendary figure rather than as a historical individual.

In this play Calderón was, as usual, concerned with illustrating an example. But, more so, his interest was focused on presenting the kind of fantastic tale that his public had an appetite for. Therefore, we cannot speak here of a dramatic chronicle in the sense of

Shakespeare's dramas about English kings. Neither can we speak of Calderón's anticipation of epic theater. The dramatic chronicle describes a historical event after the pattern of illuminated medieval chronicles whose charm consists of the fact that they depicted only the most spectacular events and allowed the observer himself to make the human connections between these events. Certainly Calderón's *Daughter of Air* is a naive dramatic tale, but the historical aspect is not so important as the adventurous life of its heroine. The historical consequencs of this life are only touched upon peripherally.

The beginning of the play lies in the sphere of the legendary. It also shows some clear parallels to *Life Is a Dream*. Semiramis, a splendid young woman, is imprisoned inside the cave of some cliffs, which are located in an isolated wilderness. She is guarded by an old priest. Here again we find the theme of the human being dressed in fur pelts; once again we can point out this cave as the ambience for the human being who has not yet realized himself. And again the fate of this human being has been predetermined by higher powers. This time it is not the stars, to be sure, but the ancient Graeco-Roman gods, who are possibly meant to symbolize the daimonic aspect implicit in such fateful forms of predetermination.

Semiramis is the daughter of a nymph who had been violated by a shepherd. Diana, the protector of virtue, wanted to kill the fruit of this sin, but Venus, the protector of love, preserved the baby. Diana sent out her obedient four-legged animals to tear Semiramis apart; Venus sent out her birds to nourish the baby with milk and "milklike" foods. Venus is victorious, but announces at the same time that this child will one day become the scourge of mankind. Therefore, like the king in *Life Is a Dream*, she arranges to have the child held prisoner in a lonely region, far apart from all human contact. So much for the play's legendary context.

The content of the play is briefly as follows: Menon, the commander-in-chief of the victorious King Ninus of Assyria, discovers the prisoner, liberates her, and falls in love with her. Fearing to lose her, he begs his prince that he be permitted to live with her apart from the world. In his appeal to the king, Menon describes Semiramis in such glowing colors that Ninus himself, through the mere words of the tale, falls in love with her. The description of Semiramis is one of the most rich in metaphors in Calderón's entire work.

Fate decrees that Semiramis one day save the king from plunging into an abyss while hunting. Now that the king sees her face to face, he sets everything on possessing her. Semiramis, who cares only about power, dissolves her connection with Menon, whom the king has had blinded out of jealousy. She now becomes Ninus's wife.

The second part of the play takes place twenty years later. Semiramis has become a powerful ruler. She has already built the glorious city of Babylon with its famous hanging gardens. The circumstances that surround the death of her royal husband are shrouded in mystery. It is said that he has been poisoned. Menon has, in the meantime, committed suicide because of her. She has her son raised far from the capital because he seems too mild for her liking.

Then Lidor, the king of the Lydians, challenges her to battle. The challenge arrives just as her maids are combing her hair. She leaves one half of her hair uncombed in order to go into battle. She takes Lidor prisoner and has him chained to the palace's gates like a dog. She then completes the arrangement of her hair by herself as if nothing had happened. At this point the people forcibly bring her son Ninyas into the city, hailing him exultantly, and she withdraws defiantly from the government. Ninyas pardons the Lydian king and begins a gentle reign. His mother energetically sets to work once again; she disguises herself as Ninyas, has the real Ninyas secretly imprisoned, and once again takes over the reins of government in his name. Since she looks just like her son, no one recognizes the deception. That mother and son never appear on the stage together seems to prove that Calderón intended to have both roles played by the same actress.

Semiramis revokes all the pardons that had been issued by her son. In the meantime, the son of the Lydian king approaches in order to free his father. Once again the queen goes out into battle. This time the fortunes of war change and she falls. In the play's grandiose death secene, as in Shakespeare's *Richard III*, the victims of her ambition for fame and glory appear before her. The particular attraction of this scene, however, is produced by the contrast between the dying heroine and the frightened gracioso, the peasant Chato, who pretends that he is dead because he is so afraid of the battle that is raging all round him. His final insight is most amusing: "I am so afraid that I do not even have the courage to escape." The people believe that Ninyas has fallen and are extremely happy when the real prince is found in the palace. The play ends in peace between the enemies, and the indispensable final marriage.

Critics have tended to consider *The Daughter of Air* as the counterpart to *Life Is a Dream*. The beginning of the play invites this comparison, but the complications of the plot prevent it from functioning as a parable as *Life is a Dream* does. *Life Is a Dream* has been termed a drama of ideas, while *The Daughter of Air* has been called a drama of nature. This may indeed be correct up to a certain point. Semiramis can be seen as a human being who has given herself entirely over to nature, to demonic forces, and who has rejected the voluntary acceptance of divine grace. Such an interpretation, however, would only be justified if the audience were able to see the moment of grace that has been allowed to pass by. But such a moment is nowhere to be found. On the contrary, the spectator is left with the impression that Semiramis has been inexorably delivered up to that predetermined fate decreed by the goddess Venus. Such a conception, of course, contradicts Calderón's Christian image of the world.

If a philosophical interpretation of this play is at all permissible, it would have to be drawn from Semiramis's last words, for it is here that she recognizes her fall as the victory of Diana over Venus, that is, the victory of virtue over nature. If one chooses to, one can interpret her concluding sentence—"I was indeed the daughter of air and into the air my breath will dissolve"—as exemplifying the a-*nihil*-ation of every human being who willingly gives himself over to natural instinct, to matter, and in the process becomes equally transitory. In this case, Venus's terrible prophecy that Semiramis would become cruel and tyrannical if she were not kept imprisoned, could be interpreted in terms of the human instinctual drives that, if they are not controlled, become a terror for one's fellow human beings.

The basic idea of this play could, however, be more simply defined as the rise and fall of a tyrant, as is true of Franz Grillparzer's drama about the fortunes and end of the Bohemian King Ottokar, which, incidentally, was based on a Spanish drama written in Calderón's day.

In November 1654, the first part of *The Daughter of Air* was performed in Spain by the company of Adrian de Lopez. Under the title *The Great Queen Semiramis*, this play was performed in 1688 in Hamburg by Master Velten's troupe. It appeared in Goethe's theater in Weimar as well, but not until 1827, shortly after it had been adapted by Ernst Raupach for a performance in Berlin. In 1881, the bicentennial year of Calderón's death, *The Daughter of Air* was one of the plays performed at the Teatro Real in Madrid.

In 1958 Hans Joachim Klein produced this play in Mannheim, using a translation by Max Kommerell. It evoked little response. Klein seems to have attempted to approach the spirit of this play through expressionistic stylistic means. The Mannheim experiment has not yet been repeated.

The Mayor of Zalamea

In *The Mayor of Zalamea*, which is today considered to be Calderón's most popular drama, the basic idea is the concept of order as the protector of virtue against human passions. The play takes place in the "most Christian" Spain of the sixteenth century. It was probably written in 1642. It is said that the plot of this play can be traced back to an event that allegedly took place in 1581. According to some sources, this work is derived from the forty-seventh novella of Masuccio of Salerno (1476).

In discussions of this play one reads time and again that it is unlike any other work of Calderón. Some critics call it a revolutionary play, others a social drama. It is considered by many to be Calderón's only drama of character.

The Mayor of Zalamea does not, however, occupy an exceptional place in Calderón's oeuvre. It is, rather, only a, perhaps somewhat unusual, variation of Calderón's theater. The play is only unusual in that the

protagonist is a common man, a class usually represented only by the graciosos in Calderón's dramas.
Calderón took this episode not in order to write a
social drama but because its plot was theatrically effective. We must never forget that Calderón was first and
foremost a practitioner of the theater and that the
most essential argument in his selection of material was
that of its suitability for the stage.

It would be completely out of character if so aristocratic and loyal a follower of the king as Calderón was
suddenly revealed revolutionary sentiments. If he had
been a revolutionist at heart, it is not likely that he
would have expressed such orientation only in one
play. But aside from these considerations, a revolutionary dramatist in the Spain of Calderón's day
would have been unthinkable. The only political motif
in the play, if there is any, is Calderón's concern with
suggesting that the king make use of the help of the
lower classes against the power of the nobility in order
to strengthen his position at the center of power.

The play begins with a description of army life. Here
speaks a dramatist who is intimately acquainted with
the life of a soldier. According to a version that cannot be verified, Calderón served as a common soldier
for a long time. But even as an officer, he must have
become sufficiently acquainted with life in the bar-
racks and on the battlefield to perceive the utter hopelessness and the necessary fatalism that pervades men
who follow this calling. Calderón, who considered
being a soldier one of the first duties honor demanded
of a Spanish cavalier, was primarily an intellectual. As
such he must inevitably have recognized to what extent the military life was fraught with evil aspects.

But, as a genuine dramatist, he does not argue pro

and con. Instead he shows us the soldier's life in its total wretchedness—the indifference and the useless recalcitrance of the common soldiers, the arrogance of their superiors who often conceal this superiority behind a mask of affable condescension. Above all, Calderón reproduced the false pride of this class whose members have considered themselves better than others from time immemorial. This is the only time that one can speak of Calderón's having voiced social criticism. He revealed an unfortunate weakness in the Spanish system of justice, that is, that soldiers received far more lenient punishments for common crimes than did civilians who commit the same offenses. But the illustration of this inequity neither provides, according to everything that we know, the reason Calderón wrote this play nor does it signify the essential of the ideas involved.

The play opens with a vivid presentation of the soldier's life, complete with the presence of a female camp follower. The theatergoer is then offered a scene that introduces Don Mendo and Nuño, who are another version of that immortal pair, Don Quixote and Sancho Panza. We then learn that the soldiers are to be lodged in the village of Zalamea, to await the arrival of Don Lope, the general. Captain Álvaro is to be lodged in the house of a wealthy farmer, Pedro Crespo. Crespo cautiously conceals his beautiful daughter Isabel on the upper floor of his house. But Álvaro, who wishes to become acquainted with Isabel, contrives to get into her room by feigning a quarrel and mock pursuit of another soldier.

The scene is interrupted by the arrival of Don Lope. He learns how matters stand and takes Álvaro's place in Crespo's house. A good relationship immediately springs up between the general, whom Calderón presents as an old, basically good-natured fire-eater, and Crespo. While Álvaro serenades Isabel, the two old men, who hear it as they sit together in the house, refuse to admit to each other their annoyance about it.

Later that night Don Lope orders Álvaro to leave Zalamea early the following morning. But Álvaro returns secretly to the village, and after Don Lope's departure he abducts Isabel. The old father, who pursues Álvaro and his comrades, is overpowered and bound to a tree, and Isabel is violated by the ruthless Álvaro.

Until this point everything that has passed is essentially theatrical—a colorful succession of scenes, relaxed by the songs of the camp follower and the funny dialogue of Don Mendo and Nuño, who turn up time and again because the knight of the sad countenance is unhappily in love with Isabel.

In the third act the themes that have so far been merely suggested become intensified to develop a tragedy of honor. The scene opens with Isabel lamenting her fate in a moving monologue, which Edward Fitzgerald, famous for his translation of Omar Khayyám's *Rubáiyát*, considered "worthy of Antigone." She finds her father in chains and liberates him. To his misfortune Álvaro has been brought to the village by his comrades because he has been wounded by Isabel's brother. His destiny is sealed by the fact that Crespo has just been elected mayor by the villagers. (As mayor he will administer justice.) At the same time news is received that the king will arrive in Zalamea that very evening. Álvaro contemptuously shrugs aside the threat of arrest on the grounds that he is subject only to military jurisdiction.

Crespo begs Álvaro on his knees to restore his daughter's injured honor by marrying her. Only after Álvaro contemptuously rejects this plea does Crespo as judge have him imprisoned. But he also has his own son Juan arrested because Juan has wounded an officer in the king's army. When Don Lope learns that a peasant has had a captain in his command put into prison, he hurries back to the village and issues a command to have the village reduced to ashes in order to free his officer.

At this point in the situation the king arrives. He asks for a report on the whole affair. His decision is that while Crespo is fundamentally in the right, Álvaro must be tried in a military court. But the king arrives too late. A gate is opened, and the theatergoer sees the captain who has been garroted. The king then declares that since the verdict was just, he will overlook the question of jurisdiction. He appoints Crespo to a lifelong term as mayor. Juan, freed from jail, is taken into the army by Don Lope, who has actually been on Crespo's side all along. Isabel goes into a convent.

Concealed behind this plot, which quite understandably has been interpreted by many modern directors as a revolutionary play or as a drama of character and a play portraying contemporary mores, is Calderón's basic view of life as illustrated in his other plays.

Calderón is not concerned with defending a particular class. Neither is his condemnation of military privilege of primary importance. Rather, as in *The Surgeon of His Honor* and in *The Painter of His Dishonor*, he is concerned with the preservation of unsullied honor. He illustrates its religious significance by showing how secular laws can be justly broken when one's honor has to be vindicated. The religious law prevails over the secular one. Even a peasant may dare to disregard the rights of the military caste in order to avenge the honor of his violated daughter. If a cause other than honor were involved, however much such a cause might have outraged our contemporary sense of justice, the king would have condemned Crespo's intervention as being illegitimate. This and only this is the basic idea of the play. It is a new variation on the drama of honor, one that was particularly effective for Calderón's contemporaries because he dramatizes the idea that the value placed on honor is so high that one is permitted for its sake to put aside considerations of social class.

Critics have also been unable to bring *The Mayor of Zalamea* into harmony with the Christian world view. They see in this play an almost Old Testament glorification of the idea of revenge, one that contradicts the teachings of Christ. When this play is examined carefully, this argument does not hold. We must remember that Crespo was not directly avenging himself. On the contrary, he tries to persuade Álvaro to redeem his daughter's honor by marrying her, thereby demonstrating enormous, almost superhuman powers of self-conquest. He offers Álvaro all his material goods, even the prerogative of selling himself and his son into slavery. If Álvaro had agreed to this offer, the Christian rule of life would have been restored. Crespo begs his enemy on his knees, which is tantamount to offering him the other cheek. Only after Álvaro scornfully rejects his plea does Crespo condemn him to death.

Calderón has skillfully allowed Crespo the father to become the local administer of justice. The death sentence is pronounced not by Crespo the father but by

Crespo the judge. Revenge becomes a legal verdict. Crespo the judge also has his own son jailed, because Juan wanted to save his sister's honor through the use of force. Only when we keep this development in the plot clearly in mind are we able to see the essential point of this drama.

It is true that Calderón did not in any other of his plays so individualize his characters. This does not mean, however, that we are dealing here with a drama of character in the Shakespearean sense. For the plot does not develop out of the characters. Rather the characters subordinate themselves to a higher law, which, as is so often true in Calderón's works, presents itself through the concept of honor.

The conclusion of the play, the timely appearance of the king, is a debated matter. (Though too late to save Álvaro's life, he saves the village from the violence and fire ordered by Don Lope.) This ending is above all great theater—the appearance of the king has a great theatrical effect. But it has greater significance than this. The appearance of the king has already been prepared. Time and again we hear that the king is on his way to being crowned king of Portugal and will pass through Zalamea on his way to Lisbon. In other words, he is an invisible presence, a character, even in the first acts of the play. That he arrives in person at the critical moment is a dramatic device.

That he must appear represents an inner necessity because it is he alone, as both the highest secular authority and the representative of God on earth, who can settle a dispute for which laws as they exist are insufficient. Without the king's intervention, the law would have been on the side of the military, in spite of all moral considerations. But the king does not nullify this law; on the basis of this unpredecented case, he does not decree a new law. What he does do is to uphold in this one case the spirit of a form of justice higher than the law of the country. In Calderón's age, the king was venerated as having godlike qualities. He represented for them the incarnation of judicial reason.

The premiere of *The Mayor of Zalamea* took place in 1643. The play has been produced in Paris ever since 1772 under the title *The Peasant Magistrate* in an adaptation by the actor and revolutionist Jean Marie Collot d'Herbois. The first known German performance of this play, entitled *Magistrate Graumann, or Incidents on a March*, was offered in 1778 in Hamburg by Friedrich Ludwig Schröder. Three years later, the Vienna Burgtheater offered its version, entitled *The Upper Magistrate and the Soldiers*. In 1782 another version was produced in Paris; this version, prepared by Faur, was known as *Isabelle and Fernand*. Throughout the nineteenth century, this work was one of the most frequently performed plays in European theater. The role of Crespo, the mayor, became increasingly one of those parts eagerly sought after by actors.

Ernst Legal's 1937 production in Berlin's Schillertheater is worthy of being noted primarily because of Heinrich George's achievement as Crespo. Another interesting German production is the one offered by Dietrich Haugk in Stuttgart in the 1955–56 season. Georg Richter's "simultaneous stage" was used here and fitted out with many unusual effects. The Spanish atmosphere was consciously emphasized. Despite the naturalness of the language and the gesture, this production was strictly stylized. In the next year, Haugk produced the play for a second time in Düsseldorf. Even more than in his Stuttgart version, Haugk attempted to work out the essential aspects of the plot by means of strict stylization; the result was a "somewhat intellectualized, but crystal-clear" production. Critics spoke of a "reflection of the natural in the light of the supernatural." In Haugk's hands it became a "play about meaning"; that is to say, a play about the meaning of order in a world of passions.

In contrast to the 1937 Berlin production and to the conceptual and rather sober 1957 Düsseldorf version, Gustav Rudolf Sellner produced *The Mayor of Zalamea* in Darmstadt, in the 1958–59 season, as a cloak-and-sword comedia.

To what extent German actors playing Crespo still stand in the shadow of Heinrich George is best demonstrated by the very different interpretation of Crespo offered by the actor Jean Vilar, who played it at the Festival of Avignon in 1961. This production was soon after offered by the Théâtre National Populaire in Paris. Vilar's Crespo had nothing of the primitive peasant in him, neither externally nor internally. As Vilar played him, Crespo was restrained, tense; all actions and emotions were held in check. This Crespo was "the true preserver of a higher law against brute force."

In Ulrich Erfurth's staging of the play in 1961 in Hamburg, Spanish sensuality is emphasized. Hermann Schomberg interpreted Crespo as a "self-sufficient, peasantlike patriarch." The stage sets were essentially realistic and their colorful nature corresponded to the concept of the production as a whole.

In the same year Sellner produced the work once again, this time in the Schillertheater in Berlin. Despite the tautness of the production as a whole, Sellner this time presented a "theater of showing," in the baroque sense of the term.

An opera, based on this play, *Pedro Crespo* by Arthur Piechler, had its premiere in Augsburg in 1947.

The Mayor of Zalamea has been produced only on a few occasions in the United States: in 1903 a production was staged at the Pabst Theater in New York by the stock company; in 1907, at the Irving Place German Theatre in New York by the German Theatre; and in 1917, at Cohan's Grand Opera House in Chicago.

In January 1946 the Readers Theater conducted a kind of experiment with *The Mayor of Zalamea*, using a translation by Edward Fitzgerald, at New York's Majestic Theater. James Light directed the presentation. It was the intention of the Readers Theater to simply offer a reading of a play seldom revived, and to prove that it was possible to make a reading of a play dramatic and exciting. No properties, costumes, or scenery were used; the actors simply read the parts.

Reaction to the experiment was mixed. The actress Miss Fania Marinoff claimed, "I was completely thrilled; I *saw* the play, I didn't merely *hear* it; it had all the force, the power, the illusion, the terror of a full-fledged production." But George Jean Nathan, writing in the *New York Journal-American* on 4 February 1946, was of a different opinion:

> It is, of course, quite possible that the reading of the classics by expert actors expertly directed might be productive of satisfactory results. . . . But unless any such enterprise is conducted at top levels it must inevitably fail. . . . The voices of the

readers must thus have the drive and eloquence of actors in the full-fledged medium. The pantomime must under the limited circumstances be superior. The power of suggestion must be even more greatly superior. With the pictorial attributes of the stage lacking, with suggestive scenery (even drapes) and lighting and music in abeyance, the challenge of illusion becomes bitter. Unless that challenge is met, what results is theatrical and dramatic bastardy.

In 1953, Alejandro Ulloa and his troupe presented *The Mayor of Zalamea* and *Life Is a Dream* in Spanish at the Broadhurst Theater in New York. Ulloa himself played the principal role in both dramas.

The Great World Theater

Calderón wrote the *auto sacramental* entitled *The Great World Theater* when he was seventy-five years old. Of all the works of this genre, it is the one most frequently performed.

There is no consensus as to the origin of the *autos sacramentales*. The medieval mystery play, the morality play, the dance of death—they are all assumed to be sources of the *auto*. Characteristic of the *auto* is its particular function as a Corpus Christi play as well as the practice of presenting the sacrifice of the mass as its climax and termination. The essential differences between Calderón's *auto* and the earlier religious plays lies, above all, in Calderón's attempt to represent theological matters through visual equivalents, that is, to make them comprehensible to an unlettered public.

The religious theater of the Middle Ages was as naive as its public; it was purely religious theater, a form of worship, as it were. Conversely, the morality play was consciously didactic and moralizing. The depiction of philosophical or theological speculation was alien to both these medieval forms. But even the basic aim of Calderón's *auto*, a hymn to the eucharist, is less the expression of a religious experience than it is the fruit of speculative thought. The doctrines of Augustine and Thomas Aquinas, as well as the conflicting ideas about the eucharist within the Spanish universities during Calderón's time, were not only present in Calderón's mind as he wrote but were actually converted into an essential element of the play itself.

The Great World Theater is considered to represent the quintessence of seventeenth-century Catholicism. Everything that Calderón wrote, *The Great World Theater* in particular, basically expresses the spirit of his age. Calderón, who was not only a great dramatist but also a significant thinker, astounds the modern theatergoer by the fact that he could function in so decisive a way only as the representative of a prevailing world view. This is because we tend to forget that Spain in Calderón's day was still in the Middle Ages, despite the discovery of America and the phenomenon of baroque art. It had not faced the skepticism of the Renaissance and the Reformation. It was the task of the medieval writer not to rediscover the world but only to represent it as it was from the very beginning, though in ever new images. Thus, the central question was not: How do I give life meaning? A goal? The question was: What does destiny want of me? Or, in other words: We are here not in order to seek God but in order to be found by Him. The initiatives lie with the higher power; it is given to us only to perceive at the right time those opportunities the higher power offers us.

The Abbot of Einsiedeln, Ignatius Staub, one of the

founders of the famous Swiss festivals, called Calderón's *Great World Theater* a *memento mori* sermon. One can hold this opinion with some justification, but one must also add that Calderón's theatrical genius did not lag behind his religious genius, that it perhaps even overshadowed the latter. Every bit of didacticism in this work is subsumed into his artistry.

The idea of viewing the world as a theater is not one of Calderón's own inventions. This idea, present in the works of classical antiquity, appears more frequently in the literature of the sixteenth and seventeenth centuries. It is possible that Calderón adapted his subject from that of the satirist Quevedo. It is in *The Great World Theater* that God makes his first appearance as a theatrical director, who, like Calderón himself, is a dramatist as well.

In a powerful overture, which is a poetic recapitulation of the act of creation, the Master summons the World. He wants to have a play presented on her meadows. His own thoughts are to become alive. But already here philosophy is dissolved into baroque theatricality: this Master resembles Calderón's earthly king in that he wishes to arrange a festival in order to give praise to his own power and glory. Life as a festival is the baroque variation of the old theme of the world as a stage. But Calderón immediately returns to his basic idea: this festival with its theatrical performance is only possible because all of life is a game. Earthly reality is illusion. Everything that the World gives to the individual players, all the costumes and the stage properties, are only loans. All the honors that men gain and all the labors they carry out are only properties of the roles that will be taken from them when the play is over.

The yet unborn, who are all alike, appear. It is the Master who distributes their roles to them: King, Beauty, Peasant, Beggar, Rich Man, Wise Man. As in real theater, some players are satisfied with their roles, some are not. But what is decisive here, as in real theater, is not the roles themselves but the way in which they are played: "Do What Is Right—God Reigns Over You!" is the title of the play to be performed, which also signifies the instructions for these actors. The Master promises to invite the actor who plays his role well to his table after the performance is over. There are dramatic antagonists in this work, just as there are in all of Calderón's works—the free will of the human being and divine grace. While free will is merely mentioned here and does not appear as an allegory, as it does in the other *autos*, divine grace is personified. It is a marvelous idea of this man of the theater to have the function of grace incorporated in the role of the Prompter. Here, as in the real theater, not all the actors listen to the words of the Prompter; some prefer to speak their own text.

When the players are one by one called away from the stage, they must return their costumes and their properties to the World. The result is that no one seems any longer to be that person whom his stage role signified; these characters are once again only human beings and as such they are all equal. The first to be invited to the divine meal are the Beggar and the Monk (the Wise Man) because both have renounced illusion already while on earth, the one because he has accepted his fate as a poor man, the other because he voluntarily removed himself from the world's illusions. At the plea of the Monk, who also represents the church, the King is pardoned because he once saved the Monk from disaster while the Monk was still on earth. Beauty and the Peasant must still go through purgatory; only the Rich Man may not eat at the Master's table.

What seems severe in the extreme to our sensibility today is the fate of the child who is never to be born, who must reach the bitterly sad conclusion: "Pain and joy are everywhere, only for me there is neither pain nor joy." Here Calderón presents a variation of that statement found in *Life Is a Dream* to the effect that guilt consists in having been born. It is in this sense that the Master says to the child: "Guiltless, yet born in guilt, no reward or punishment for you."

Perhaps Calderón wished to express in the child's cries of despair, which sound like dissonances amid the exultation of those who have been redeemed, his own pain-filled response to a religious doctrine whose severity he finds incomprehensible. Although this point of view will hardly find acceptance among literary critics, its truth becomes apparent when one sees this play performed. It may also be noted that the child's fate contradicts the introductory words of the play, in which the Master chooses man as the actor in his festival because he is the most skillful being in his creation. At this point there is not yet any indication of guilt without sin.

The staging of the *autos* becomes clear to us by an examination of the construction of *The Great World Theater*. The stage is divided into two spheres, the world and heaven. Before the human beings act upon the stage of the world, it is covered by a gray curtain. Heaven becomes visible in all its theatrical glory only when a curtain is raised. The simple mechanics of the old Spanish stage have been developed here into a great baroque outdoor theater.

Above and beyond all its details, *The Great World Theater* can be allowed to stand as the symbolic representation of a view of life in which not only is the world presented as theater but the theater as such signifies the world. Both represent the great and glorious illusion that man loves with a passion, from which he can liberate himself only by a higher passion, the passion for truth.

The Great World Theater had its premiere in Seville in 1675.

In the 1920s Peter Erkelenz, the director of the Calderón Society in Germany, had the idea of performing his work in front of the Church of the Pilgrims in Einsiedeln, Switzerland. This church, together with its adjoining rectory, is the only baroque building north of the Alps that resembles the Escorial both in its basic outline and in its construction. This production was first offered in 1924 under Erkelenz's direction. He also played the role of the Master himself. Five hundred amateur players and one hundred technical assistants participated in this performance. It was produced on a stage of Erkelenz's own design, which was set up in front of the church.

It was not until 1930 that the church itself was more directly included in the action of the play. Only under the direction of the Swiss scholar of theatrical history Oskar Eberle (1935, 1937, 1950), however, was a baroque solution attempted. Eberle allowed the church to "play its role" directly, both optically and acoustically. He made use of its bells, illuminated win-

dows, and finally the door that opened in a theatrical
fashion when the Master walked out of it. He ex-
hausted all the effective theatrical possibilities suggested within the play. He allowed the unborn beings
to arrange a race for the good roles. He had the
World together with her retinue flee from Death.
The World's companions were earth demons, who all
wore Swiss folk masks. In this way Eberle combined
the baroque work of art with indigenous customs. At
the end, he also included the audience in the play by
having them all join in the singing of a concluding
chorale. Eberle offered the play as an oratorio rather
than a mime. The play became a Swiss tourist attraction.

It is to be expected that opposing voices would
make themselves heard after World War II as a result
of the changes that had taken place in our religious
and artistic sensibilities. These voices rejected the
pomp and circumstance of this production. The Viennese director Gustav Manker attempted to stage this
same play in the Wasserkirche in Zurich. Approaching
the play solely from its spiritual content, he trimmed
away all the external effects. But his production could
not compete with the amateur performances given in
Einsiedeln.

In 1955, Karlheinz Stroux began his career as the
manager of the Düsseldorf theater with his version of
Calderón's *Great World Theater*. This production
employed Eichendorff's translation, which was also
being used for the Einsiedeln production. Stroux presented the play as a "carousel of the world"; brilliant
choreography presented the events in concentrated
form. Between the gate of birth and the gate of death
was spread the tapestry-like carpet of life.

A Salzburg Mysterienbühne (a theater for the production of religious mystery plays) produced the work in 1959, using an adaptation by Ludwig Drexler. Drexler transposed the action to that of the twentieth century.

BIBLIOGRAPHY

1. WORKS BY CALDERÓN

Absalom's Locks—Cabellos de Absalom.

Belshazzar's Feast—La cena de Baltasar. Translation by Denis Florence McCarthy, in *Calderón de la Barca: Six Plays*, revised and edited by Henry W. Wells, New York: Las Américas, 1961.

Beware of Still Waters—Guárdate de la agua mansa. Translation, "Beware of Smooth Water," by Edward Fitzgerald, in *Eight Dramas of Calderón*, New York: Macmillan, 1906; reprinted New York: Dolphin Books, 1961.

The Constant Prince—El príncipe constante. Translation by Denis Florence McCarthy, in *Calderón de la Barca: Six Plays*, revised and edited by Henry W. Wells, New York: Las Américas, 1961.

The Daughter of Air—La hija del aire.

The Devotion to the Cross—La devoción de la cruz. Translation by Edwin Honig, in *Calderón: Four Plays*, New York: Hill & Wang, 1961.

Divine Orpheus—Divino Orfeo.

141

Faithful Shepherd—El pastor fido.

The Game of Hide-and-Seek—Escondido.

The Game of Love and Fortune—Lances de amor.

The Ghostly Lover—El galán fantasma.

The Grand Duke of Gandia—El gran duque de Gandia.

The Great World Theater—El gran teatro del mundo. Translation, "The Great Theatre of the World," by Mack Hendricks Singleton, in *Masterpieces of the Spanish Golden Age*, edited by Angel Flores, New York: Rinehart, 1957.

A House with Two Entrances Is Hard to Protect—Casa con dos puertas, mala es de guardar. Translation, "A House with Two Doors Is Difficult to Guard," by Edwin Muir, in *Tulane Drama Review* 7 (1963):157–217.

In This Life Everything Is True and Everything Is False—En esta vida todo es verdad y todo mentira.

Jealousy, The Greatest Monster—El mayor mónstruo los celos.

Life Is a Dream—La vida es sueño. Verse translation by Roy Campbell, in *The Classic Theatre III: Six Spanish Plays*, edited by Eric Bentley, New York: Doubleday (Anchor), 1959. See also *Life Is a Dream*, translated by William E. Colford, New York: Barron, 1958.

The Loud Secret—El secreto a voces. Translation, "The Secret in Words," by Denis Florence McCarthy, in *Dramas I, by Calderón*, London: Dolman, 1853.

Love after Death—Amar después de la muerte. Verse translation by Roy Campbell, in *The Classic Theatre III: Six Spanish Plays*, edited by Eric Bentley, New York: Doubleday (Anchor), 1959.

Love, The Greatest Enchantment—El mayor encanto amor. Translation by Denis Florence McCarthy, in *Calderón's Dramas*, London: Longmans, Green, 1861.

The Mayor of Zalamea—El alcalde de Zalamea. Translation by Edwin Honig, in *Calderón: Four Plays*, New York: Hill & Wang, 1961.

The Merchant of Women—La niña de Gomez Arias.

The Mysteries of the Sacred Mass—Mistérios de la missa.

The Painter of His Dishonor—El pintor de su deshonra. Translation by Edward Fitzgerald, in *Eight Dramas of Calderón*, New York: Macmillan, 1906; reprinted New York: Dolphin Books, 1961.

The Phantom Lady—La dama duende. Translation by Edwin Honig, in *Calderón: Four Plays*, New York: Hill & Wang, 1961.

Poisoned and Cured—Veneno y la triaca.

The Schism in England—La cisma de Inglaterra.

Secret Vengeance for Secret Insult—A secreto agravio, secreta venganza. Translation by Edwin Honig, in *Calderón: Four Plays*, New York: Hill & Wang, 1961.

The Surgeon of His Honor—El médico de su honra. Translation by Roy Campbell, *The Surgeon of His Honour*, with introduction by E. W. Hesse, Madison: University of Wisconsin Press, 1960.

Tomorrow Is a New Day—Mañana sera.

The Wonder-working Magician—El mágico prodigioso. Translation by Denis Florence McCarthy, in *Calderón de la Barca: Six Plays*, revised and edited by Henry W. Wells, New York: Las Américas, 1961. See also translation fragments by Percy Bysshe Shelley, in *The Classic Theatre III: Six*

Spanish Plays, edited by Eric Bentley, New York: Doubleday (Anchor), 1959.

You Can't Play with Love—No hay burlas con el amor.

Zenobia—La gran Cenobia.

2. EDITIONS OF CALDERÓN'S COLLECTED WORKS

Obras. 5 vols. 1636–77.

Obras. Edited by Juan de Vera Tassis. 9 vols. 1682–91.

Autos sacramentales. Edited by P. Pando Mier. 6 vols. 1717.

Comedias completas. Edited by J. E. Hartzenbusch. 4 vols. 1848–50.

Obras completas. I, *Dramas.* Edited by Luis Astrana Marín. Madrid, 1951.

Obras completas. II, *Comedias.* Edited by Angel Valbuena Briones. Madrid, 1956.

3. WORKS ABOUT CALDERÓN

Dunn, P. N. "Honour and the Christian Background in Calderón." *Bulletin of Hispanic Studies* 37 (1960): 75–105.

Fitzmaurice-Kelly, James. *Chapters on Spanish Literature.* New York: Kraus Reprint, 1908.

Friedrich, Hugo. *Der fremde Calderón.* Freiburg, 1966.

Honig, Edwin. *Calderón and the Seizures of Honor.* Cambridge: Harvard University Press, 1972.

Jones, C. A. "Honor in *El alcalde de Zalamea.*" *Modern Language Review* 50 (1955):444–49.

Kommerell, Max. *Beiträge zu einem deutschen Calderón.* Frankfurt on the Main, 1946.

Madariaga, Salvador de. *Shelley and Calderón.* Port Washington, N.Y.: Kennikat Press, 1965.

Menéndez y Pelayo, M. *Calderón y su teatro.* Madrid, 1881.

Oppenheimer, M. "The Baroque Impasse in the Calderonian Drama." *Publications of the Modern Language Association of America* 65 (1950):1146–65.

Parker, A. A. *The Allegorical Drama of Calderón: An Introduction to the Autos Sacramentales.* Oxford: Dolphin, 1943.

———. "The Approach to the Spanish Drama of the Golden Age." *Tulane Drama Review* 4 (1959).

Sloman, A. E. *The Sources of Calderon's "El príncipe constante."* 1950.

———. *The Dramatic Craftsmanship of Calderón.* Oxford: Dolphin, 1958.

Trench, Richard Chenevix. *Calderón, His Life and Genius, with Specimens of His Plays.* New York: Redfield, 1856.

Valbuena Prat, Angel. *Calderón, su personalidad, su arte dramático, su estilo y sus obras.* Barcelona: Editorial Juventud, 1941.

Wardropper, Bruce W. "The Unconscious Mind in Calderón's *El pintor de su deshonra.*" *Hispanic Review* 18 (1950):285–301.

———, ed. *Critical Essays on the Theatre of Calderón.* New York: New York University Press, 1965.

Wier, L. E. *The Ideas Embodied in the Religious Drama of Calderón.* Lincoln: University of Nebraska Studies, 1940.

Wilson, E. M. "The Four Elements in the Imagery of Calderón." *Modern Language Review* 31 (1936): 34–47.

INDEX